THE SCIENTIFIC BASIS OF
HEALTH SERVICES

THE SCIENTIFIC BASIS OF HEALTH SERVICES

Edited by

MICHAEL PECKHAM
*Director of Research and Development for the
Department of Health*

RICHARD SMITH
Editor, BMJ

First published in 1996
by the BMJ Publishing Group, BMA House, Tavistock Square,
London WC1H 9JR

British Library Cataloguing in Publication Data

A catalogue record for this book is available from the British Library

ISBN 0-7279-1029-9

Typeset, printed and bound in Great Britain
by Derry & Sons Limited, Nottingham

Contents

Preface

Progress in medicine and science and anticipated advances over the next decade offer the prospect of far reaching changes in health care. However, although science exerts a powerful influence on health services and health is the explicit or assumed raison d'etre of a substantial part of science, overall the connection between the two cultures has been weak, sometimes with conflict, despite a common purpose. Thus the task of organising services is complicated by the state of continuous change provoked by scientific innovation, and the resulting ambivalence towards new interventions is matched by the frustration scientists may experience in trying to introduce research findings into practice.

It is clear that a fresh approach to the relationship between science and health services is both timely and necessary. Advances relevant to health are being made across a broad range of biological, physical, and social sciences with blurring of conventional subject boundaries, the formation of interspecialty links, and the emergence of new areas of research. This trend will force us to reappraise the relevance of existing subject headings, the arguments for juxtaposing research institutes and hospitals, and the relationship between universities and health services. It brings under scrutiny conventional ways of organising science in relation to health care and raises the need for new approaches to the relationship between health services and health care industries.

The scope of science and medical practice also focuses attention on the nature of contemporary clinical research, which in turn raises questions about how to define the experimental component of health services where increasingly the emphasis will be on the use of methods that have been fully validated.

At the same time scientific methods and concepts will be drawn on to a much greater extent as health services are restructured to make them more flexible, effective, affordable, and responsive to patients. In the latter context a significant new variable will be a better informed public who understand, as well as influence, what is offered to them. More emphasis will need to be given by health services and by the scientific community to short and medium term foresight, particularly in growth areas such as genetics and information and communication science.

Health sectors in different countries will devise distinctive responses to the uses of science in the formation of health policy. The result will be diverse approaches and the comparative aspects of policy will merit more attention if benefit is to be derived from health policy "experiments" conducted throughout the world.

In response to the challenge of realigning the science and health sectors, from 1991 a new strategy was introduced in the UK aimed at creating a fundamentally different relationship between the NHS and science and technology. Research and development was established as a core function of the NHS, a national infrastructure was set in place, and new relationships were developed with the Medical Research Council, the charities, industry, and the Higher Education Funding Council responsible for core funding of universities.

A national standing group on health technology was created and a wide ranging programme of technology assessment was launched. A technology scanning function was set up to alert the health service to incipient new developments.

The UK Cochrane Centre and NHS Centre for Reviews and Dissemination were established to undertake the task of mobilising and analysing for practical use the vast backlog of research data of great potential value to the health service.

Research oriented towards clearly defined priorities was supported in a wide range of areas including mental health, cardiovascular disease and stroke, asthma, cancer, mother and child health, the implementation of research findings, the interface between primary and secondary care, and physical and complex disabilities. A programme aimed at devising new research and development methods was introduced and initiatives were launched to introduce research based information into clinical guidelines and into the contracts between health authorities and hospitals. A start was made on the important issue of involving lay people in health service issues as well as in research. A new approach to the education and training of medical and non-medical staff was introduced with the establishment of the centres for evidence based medicine in Oxford and evidence based child health in London.

Of fundamental importance were the steps taken to introduce a new funding mechanism whereby the resources for health care and the funding of research and development were clearly separated. These arrangements were designed to provide a secure basis for the conduct of clinical research in hospitals and primary care and to support technology assessment and health services research more generally.

The conference entitled the Scientific Basis of Health Services held in London in October 1995 had its origin in the experience gained over the previous five years in setting up the NHS research and development programme. As a first attempt to explore the wider relationship between science and health services, the conference itself was an experiment. The results were encouraging with over 1000 delegates attending from more than 40 countries reflecting interests from about the same number of different areas of activity and specialisation.

This book includes a selection of papers presented at the conference. It is not meant to be comprehensive but serves to stimulate new thinking and to illustrate the rich diversity of issues that come under the general heading "scientific basis of health services".

Professor Sir Michael Peckham
Director, Science and Health Forum, University College London
Director of Research and Development, NHS, 1991–1995

February 1996

1 Foresight of advances in science and technology

RICHARD B SYKES

In recent years the providers of health care, whether in the public or private sectors, have been faced with some radical changes in the society they serve and some important developments in the way that health care is delivered to communities. They have had to come to terms with rapid advances in science and technology affecting the way in which human diseases are diagnosed and treated. These changes have already started to have an impact not only on the health care providers but also on those industries, such as the biopharmaceutical and diagnostic industries, which supply them.

I would like first to discuss some of the pressures now being experienced by health care systems and then examine areas of science and technology that have the capacity or promise to contribute to meeting the present and future demands for better treatments, better medicines, and better processes. It must also be accepted, however, that there will be problems to be faced in bringing scientific and technological advances to bear effectively on the provision of health care.

The pressures on health care providers

In most developed societies the population has come to expect high standards of provision of care. To a large extent this is due to the success of the health services themselves and to progress in medical and surgical science and practice but also to the efforts of the pharmaceutical industry. Over the past 40 to 50 years serious or life threatening infectious diseases have been eradicated or

1

controlled by use of vaccines and effective antibiotics. Other chronic conditions can be alleviated by the use of medicines such as anti-inflammatory, antihypertensive, and antiasthmatic drugs. Similarly there have been impressive developments in surgery, such as total joint replacement in arthritis, bypass surgery in heart disease, and transplantation for the replacement of failing organs. Thus there is an expectation that those responsible for health services should be able to investigate and treat the disease challenges of our own time, such as malignancies and degenerative diseases, effectively by using state of the art facilities and methods. At the same time that increasing demands are being made the costs involved in the provision of health services are also rising, placing considerable strains on the system. The capital outlay required to provide modern facilities is an ongoing and heavy expense. Providers are also facing escalating costs of obtaining the services and labour they require.

One of the greatest pressures on health care systems, however, arises from demographic changes. The populations of most developed nations are aging. In England and Wales population statistics indicate that from the 1940s there has been an accelerated rise in the number of over 60s, and this increase is projected to continue into the next century. These changes are due in large measure to the advances in medical and surgical treatment and in improvements in public health and health care provision. A different spectrum of disease is assuming prominence, in which diseases affecting the over 60s, such as malignancies, degenerative arthritides, and neurodegenerative conditions, are placing an increasing burden on the community. Another consequence of this demographic trend is the decreasing ratio of earners to non-earners in the population, thus, if present trends continue, by 2020 it is estimated that there will be only about two earners per retired person. Revenue available for the public sector health services is therefore under pressure. Providers of health care are thus faced with managing the health problems of an aging population against a background of limited available funds. Their problem is therefore to find new ways of delivering effective care.

In the United Kingdom and elsewhere various solutions have been proposed, debated, and sometimes implemented. For the most part these are aimed at the reduction of costs of providing health care by imposing limitations on the services or medicines to be made available, by rationing access, or by increasing revenue through contributions from patients. Such steps could be expected to result in reduced costs, but they will be modest and certainly painful for both patient and doctor. An alternative approach, being pioneered by health care organisations, mainly in the United States, is through disease management; an approach not focused solely on monetary cost saving but on understanding diseases and examining the outcomes of therapeutic interventions to optimise treatment and obtain the best outcome. Money is saved by better informed use of available resources operating through the whole system of health care management rather than picking off individual components. This is an approach with the potential to attack the root causes of rising health care costs.

Solutions from science and technology

The past two decades have seen major advances in science and technology. The explosion of biological knowledge is providing an insight into the cellular and molecular basis of disease. Advances in understanding of disease processes will contribute to improvements in the management of human disease. They are already providing the health care professions and the biopharmaceutical and diagnostic industries with new capabilities. Such new understanding of the basis of common diseases, together with advances in other branches of science and technology, will put the biopharmaceutical industry in a good position to discover or design new medicines capable of curing or at least arresting the course of these diseases. New diagnostic agents based on advances in molecular biology, biotechnology, or monoclonal antibody technology are bringing precision and speed to routine diagnostic tests.

The technological revolution has provided powerful means of communicating through cable, optical fibres, and by satellite—making it possible to send data instantaneously around the world. Telemedicine—once science fiction—is now fact and can provide new methods of health care delivery. Advances in electronics and computing have provided robotic methods of carrying out tasks many more times efficiently than was hitherto possible. For example, they open the way to high throughput screening—for new drug discovery or for detecting diseases in populations; speeding up chemical syntheses. Computerised robots are now being used in surgery.

The third area in which there has been great progress is in information technology. Increased computational capacity and development of powerful database software make possible the development of international collections of accessible and analysable data. Without this capacity the human genome programme could not have been as effective as it is, and progress would have been both costly and slow. Advances in information technology also offer the opportunity to generate and develop managed health care systems.

A caveat, however, must be added. New understanding and new technological capabilities can result in precision and efficiencies in health care provision, but if they are not used wisely and implemented only after careful evaluation they will almost certainly result in increased costs.

It is possible here to review only a few of the areas in which science and technology are offering advances in the health care arena.

The biological explosion

During the past 20 years major advances in cellular and molecular biology have resulted in an explosive expansion of knowledge of biological systems that is permitting an understanding of normal and disease processes in the human body that was hitherto impossible. This is well exemplified by the human genome programme, the major international research project to identify, map, and sequence the 100 000 or so genes that make up the human genome. This immense task is made possible through the enormous expansion of our capabilities in molecular biology and biotechnology and the development of powerful interactive international databases and the communications technology which makes them accessible.

In *The Book of Man* Bodmer and McKie have described the human genome as ". . . the instruction set according to which we are all made. When we learn to read its pages and chapters we will have obtained information relevant to understanding of most diseases . . ."[1]

The programme is of importance because of the contribution it will make to the development of new diagnostics and medicines. Once genes associated with disease are identified the next step is to discover their molecular products and define their function. Then we will have new insights into various diseases and new ways of treating them. An example is the case of cystic fibrosis where it has been possible, from the discovery of the defective gene, to identify the cellular defect that gives rise to the thickened

4

bronchial mucous characteristic of that disease. The cystic fibrosis transmembrane conductance regulator, which is the product of the gene, was found to be a defective chloride channel. From this information clinical trials of gene therapy have begun, entailing the insertion of the normal gene into the cells of the respiratory tract of patients. The results of these first trials are awaited, but there is good reason to believe that gene therapy will eventually correct the molecular lesions in the lung. In severe combined immunodeficiency disease, inserting the gene for the defective enzyme, adenosine deaminase, into the patient's lymphocytes has shown clinical potential; but there are drawbacks—repeated treatments are needed as the cells containing the correct gene die out. In other diseases, such as Huntington's chorea, although the gene is identified, the gene product is not known and the means of delivering the gene to the affected cells in the brain is so far lacking.

As the understanding of the genetic basis of disease grows, so too will the capacity to bring about genetic modification of tissues or even the whole body through gene insertion or deletion. There are, however, several issues to be dealt with. A practical problem is the safe and effective delivery of the gene to its target cells. Development of methods for introducing genes into stem cells of affected cell linages would remove the need for continual treatment as cells die out; but in multigenic disorders greater understanding of the interaction between disease-associated genes and between the gene and the environment is required.

The greatest potential of the human genome programme, however, lies in its capacity to allow the identification of molecular targets against which small molecules may be directed as new medicines.

The technological revolution

Advances in many fields of technology are making or will make contributions to the more effective delivery of health care. Two will be considered here.

Development of non-invasive imaging techniques has opened up new possibilities for the detection and diagnosis of disease and also provided new tools with which to probe their underlying mechanisms. There are important human diseases that do not have an animal counterpart and whose progression cannot be studied longitudinally in patients by means of biopsy. The diseases of the brain are such conditions. By the time the pathologist sees the

5

affected tissues the changes are well advanced, the battle long over, and the original participants are long since buried. Imaging technologies—starting with x ray photography—have revealed internal structures, but the type of information that they can deliver is limited.

Recently more precise and dynamic methods, employing firstly radioscintigraphy and then positron emission tomography (PET) and magnetic resonance imaging (MRI), have been developed. These allow the visualisation not only of physical changes in the tissues during the course of disease but increasingly permit the study of biochemical and physiological processes taking place in them during normal functioning and their disturbance in disease. In the future it will be possible to couple the use of these powerful and sensitive technologies with the use of synthetic ligands for key cellular receptors. This will make it increasingly possible to understand the cellular and possibly also the molecular changes in the patient's brain and, from this information, to gain insights that may lead to the discovery of new medicines and methods of treatment and also allow the effectiveness of treatment to be monitored over time. These non-invasive imaging techniques are also now making targeted and precise surgery possible in the brain in conditions such as epilepsy.

Developments in communications technology are making it possible to link the physician's office with local and more distant hospital facilities such as the records office and diagnostic departments. Most importantly it is now possible for the general practitioner in the surgery to engage in real time consultation with specialists in the hospital to obtain advice. The consultant can also have real time access to investigations carried out in the surgery— such as electrocardiograms—and even examine the patient via a television link. It will be possible for the patient, provided with appropriate equipment, to monitor his or her own condition at home—for example, blood pressure, blood sugar concentrations, or peak air flow—with the data being provided directly into the disease management system and advice about treatment fed back to patient and doctor. Clearly the application of such technologies in the context of health care can bring added value to health services.

The information revolution

A third area in which there have been major advances is that of information technology. The impact of these advances can already be seen. The assembly of large and complex databases is now possible, drawing down information from many different sources and providing a considerable analytical power to optimise the value of the data collected. This new technology is playing a key part in the human genome programme and without it that programme would not have been able to gather the momentum it has.

Development of disease management systems is another area in which information technology, coupled with communications networks, will make an important contribution to cost effective delivery of health care. Essentially a disease management system is a communications network involving those responsible for treating and monitoring patients. It allows flow of data from clinical centres—hospital clinics, wards and laboratories, general practitioner surgeries, and pharmacies—into the data management system of the disease management organiser. The data will include diagnostic information, details of treatment regimens used, information about patient response and compliance, and any adverse reactions. All information input into the system is analysed and updated, and from outcomes analyses "best practice" guidelines for the particular disease and patient type, generated to deliver high quality outcomes at lowest possible overall cost, are fed back to the clinical centres. Further, the doctors will be provided with up to date records concerning their particular patients.

The disease management system is simply the provision of access to the cumulative "wisdom" and practices of those handling the patients and permitting this to be applied more widely in the most cost and clinically effective manner. Disease management organisers may offer broad services covering a wide spectrum of diseases or may deal with only one particular condition such as HIV, diabetes, heart failure, or asthma. Early experience with this approach in the United States is encouraging. In the case of asthma, for example, it has been found that by using a disease management system expensive hospital admissions—particularly in emergency situations—have been reduced, the emphasis being moved to primary health care. The extent of use of medicines in patients with the milder forms of the disease has increased whereas in the patients with moderate to severe disease drug use has been reduced. Overall the cost of treating asthma effectively has been significantly reduced from the normal trend. One estimate suggests savings of between $200–300 billion could be possible within the United States by implementation of disease management system approaches to health care delivery.

Some problems

From the few examples given it is clear that there is enormous potential in science and technology to bring about improvements in the delivery of health care to the patient and the provision of better treatments. There are also new issues and problems, however, that the use of new developments will raise. These must be faced if the full potential of scientific and technological advances are to be realised.

Genetic studies of diseases in populations are going to show that many common diseases are linked to particular genes. Before this genetic information can be used for new drug design or attempts at gene therapy, however, the role of genes in relation to other factors must be known. These include environmental factors, lifestyle, diet etc. The unravelling of these relations will take time and require costly epidemiological research and the development of new information technology systems to collect and analyse clinical, lifestyle, and other data from a number of centres. It will also require the large scale cooperation between major hospitals and clinics. Incidentally, data to help answer these questions could well emerge from disease management systems.

Once a clear genetic basis is established for a particular disease, screening strategies may be developed for the reduction of the disease burden in the population. Apart from questions of cost efficiency, however, there is a range of ethical and social questions to be faced. Should screening be offered only to people who are at high risk, only when pregnant or before pregnancy? Should screening be available to a wider group of people or even on a population-wide basis? Genetic screening could be effective in reducing the burden of genetic disease, but it does give rise to questions about how costs of screening should be met—by the health care provider or by the individual? If the latter, then what will be the consequences of restriction to those who can afford it and any subsequent treatment? One effect of such a policy will be the exclusion of the poorer sections of the community who can ill afford the cost burden of genetic disease.

The recent reports from the Nuffield Council on Bioethics and from the House of Commons Science and Technology Committee on Human Genetics has drawn attention to the problems for society that are likely to arise from the human genome programme. The consequences of availability of information about an individual's genetic make up, particularly when genes for disease susceptibility are involved, need to be considered in the context, for example, of the insurance industry or employment. These are not entirely new issues, they have already been encountered in the context of AIDS and HIV, but they do assume a new dimension. A difficult question also arises of whether and how to use results from genetic diagnosis in those diseases that will occur in later life and for which there is at present no treatment. For a person to know that, for example, he or she carries the gene for Huntington's chorea could become akin to a sword of Damocles.

Implementation of disease management systems could also encounter problems, but in this case they are likely to be professional or cultural ones on the part of the users of the systems. The health care professions may see the disease management systems as threats to the clinical freedom to which they have been accustomed. There will be concerns about the security and confidentiality of the information on the databases. Patients are likely to prefer contact with their doctors rather than "remote medicine" and some, particularly older people, will be unable to cope with the technology required for "self management". The health care payers, however, will want to see value and cost effectiveness in the system and this must be clearly demonstrated. Therefore the successful integration of disease management systems into health services will need care, involvement of all the parties to be engaged, and education and training of both the professionals and the patients. It will also be essential to build up a trust regarding the way in which the information held in the system is used.

Finally, it must be understood that although new scientific understanding and new technological capabilities can result in new precision and efficiencies in health care provision, they must be carefully assessed. If they are not used wisely and after proper evaluation they will result in increased costs. New medicines, new diagnostics, new techniques, and new processes must be stringently evaluated, not only for efficacy and safety—which has long been a requirement in the case of new medicines—but also for their ability to add value to the health care system as a whole. Failure to observe this is likely to lead to increased burdens being placed on health care services, already under strain, and bringing little real benefit to patients, the professions, and the providers (whether governments or private bodies).

Conclusion

Developments in science and technology have made valuable contributions to the health services, and there may be every confidence that this will continue in years to come. For maximum benefits to be realised from the development and exploitation of science and technology health care, however, it is essential that partnerships are developed. These must involve governments, the health care professions, the academic community, and the biopharmaceutical and other health care industries. We must all be prepared to recognise each other's contribution and our interdependence. If our investment of skills, time, and money is to maximise the return from these efforts we must develop new partnership approaches to ensure health care systems that give value for money and ensure the health of our communities.

1 Bodmer W, McKie R. *The book of man*. London: Little, Brown and Co, 1994.

2 Towards a paradigm for technology assessment

RENALDO N BATTISTA

Over the past decade many activities have been gathered under the expanding tent of technology assessment. This rapid growth and exuberance captures both the newness of technology assessment as a coherent topic and the hunger of decision makers for the information available from technology assessment activities. Technology assessors and their assessments now face increasingly complex demands for information regarding increasingly complex decisions. Technology assessment, if it is to be more than simply that which is done by self styled technology assessors, needs a conceptual framework, a paradigm.

In this chapter I will present my vision of health care technology assessment drawing on my teaching experience and many discussions with my students and colleagues coupled with my practical experience with several working groups and technology assessment organisations, specifically the Quebec Health Technology Assessment Council. I will define a paradigm of technology assessment through metaphors of the bridge, the tree, and the voyage of Ulysses. Establishing a paradigmatic basis for technology assessment distinct from those of science and policy making is essential for technology assessment's maturation. I have adopted a Kuhnian notion of paradigms in the sense that the paradigm of technology assessment is one that provides model problems and solutions to the community of technology assessors.

Several recurring themes occur in this book. These issues cross the nations, as we are dealing with sickness in an aging population; newer pressures of cost; and shorter hospital stays. Many issues in health care are deemed to have a scientific basis. Communication technology is playing an ever greater role in disseminating information and implementing decisions or practices shaped by such information. Throughout all of this is the trust in science, which is often perceived to be a proxy for truth, but also the recognition of its limits.

The three metaphors

I have chosen three images, whose threads I will interweave with the themes I have identified above. Through this exercise, I believe a coherent beginning for a paradigmatic view of health care technology assessment will emerge.

The bridge

Technology assessment's beginnings stem from a desire for information, usually of a technical nature and often for use by people or groups who, while responsible for decisions affecting the acquisition, use, or management of various technologies, are often not intimately familiar with the technologies. The bridge then links the world of scientific, technical knowledge with that of decision making or more broadly policy making.

While policy conjures up images of country or system level decisions made by powerful people, "policy" in health care and particularly regarding technology encompasses both these decisions and matters such as the practice patterns of physicians and the coverage decisions of private sector insurers or local health authorities. Decisions at all levels of health care systems are increasingly to be based on evidence, justified in light of evidence, or at the very least documented.

Throughout history the bridge has powerfully symbolised communication. Each of the scientific and policy realms have their rituals and one of the key roles of technology assessment is surely the establishment of a means of two directional movement that would alleviate non-comprehension which could unduly hamstring the scientist facing a government committee on health sector restructuring or the policy maker snowed under by conflicting evidence from clinical research.

Flowing from this notion of two directional movement is an important associated notion of boundaries ·and spaces. For technology assessment to contribute to decision making mutually defined spaces must exist for both realms such that the scientific work may proceed unimpeded but not uninformed by the policy process and the policy process may proceed informed but not hijacked by the reductionist tendencies of scientific inquiry. Negotiating these spaces and associated boundaries must be an ongoing part of bridge maintenance. The maintenance and improvement of the bridges between science and policy cannot be the responsibility of only one of the two joined parties. Moreover, somewhere in the interaction between science, technology assessment, and policy making there are the people who use and finance health services. I will go further and propose that the process of technology assessment, as much as it is about bringing scientists and policy makers together, is driven by a fundamental search for equity through wide sharing of information among all the people in the health care system, including the citizens themselves.

In any society or group of people some sort of decision making élite emerges and draws to itself power, typically through its ability to make decisions governing the distribution of scarce resources. Increasingly, the nature of the choices surrounding health technologies requires not only meta-analyses and cost effectiveness studies but a very human encounter with uncertainty in both patients and providers.

The tree

Technology assessment can be viewed as a tree, firmly rooted in scientific inquiry but with its foliage turned towards policy making. As labyrinthine as much of policy making may seem, it is the needs of policy makers for information that provide sunlight to the tree of technology assessment. The technology assessment process is pointless without an audience or user for information, be it patients, providers, or payers.

What then of the audiences for technology assessment, or to put it another way, is the audience but a sap for the hegemony of so called "objective" science? I believe that part of the uniqueness of technology assessment is its threat to such hegemony. Most of you I am sure can think of situations where scientific evidence pouring forth in the form of P values or bands on a gel seems so obviously powerful that great change in the experience of illness or the practice of medicine is forecast with the assurance of Biblical truth. And as several of the other chapters so clearly illustrate, in the real world, practice and, alas, the natural history of many illnesses remain resistant to such religious-like fervour.

The results of scientific inquiry generally require processing and packaging for maximum impact. Scientific results alone produce change rarely, and so called scientific evidence exerts its effects on natural history or practice only after passing through a complex sociological maze. The various branches that sprout on the tree of technology assessment act to illuminate the vastly more complex range of domains that affect the translation of scientific evidence into policy for health services. But a tree without roots cannot survive and similarly technology assessment will wither unless there is a continuing flow of high quality scientific investigation to nurture the process and to provide inputs to policy makers and increasingly, individual people.

This increasing role for individual decision makers I have alluded to earlier in the context of making choices in light of technological advances. More specifically, human genome activities and advances in molecular medicine pose questions the likes of which policy can only guide. For example, do parents wish to seek abortion knowing that their child carries a gene involved in cystic fibrosis, a disease for which life expectancy has doubled in roughly the past 15 years? Scientific wizardry and policy brilliance are of minimal value in making what are fundamentally human choices in the face of great uncertainty—technology assessment is no less helpless but does offer an avenue for organising and communicating information from many domains potentially relevant to making such choices.

The journey into the realm of decisions where both patients and providers are admitting the extent of their uncertainty is a byproduct of both the history and future of health services. Historically, a "war on mortality" has dominated medicine for much of this century. The spoils of that war are rapidly growing numbers of long living citizens, whose advancing age raises questions of quality of life and terminal care that no amount of science can answer. Looking ahead, the headlong rush into molecular biology, portrayed by its most ardent proponents as a journey to the meaning of life itself, creates unprecedented dilemmas regarding the use of DNA diagnostics and prognostic markers for illnesses for events whose occurrence may be many years away.

This journey, from a simple war on mortality, "more life at any cost", to the more involved "what quality of life and how much will it cost?" brings me to my third metaphor, that of Ulysses and his voyage home from the Trojan war.

14

Ulysses

The story of Ulysses is a great epic full of tragedy and a rather extended trip home that, passing between Sicily and mainland Italy, requires him to negotiate the straits between Scylla and Charybdis. The perils of his journey highlight the risks inherent to technology assessment as it makes its way between science and policy. The importance of bridge building and communication to the successful conclusion of technology assessment's journey cannot be overemphasised.

When Ulysses returned home he was not immediately recognised. Times and people change and it was only through the bending of the bow that people recognised him. Within the social discourse on health care there is a fundamental difference between the often sobering comments of the technology assessor regarding rationalisation and the historically triumphant flamboyance of medicine. With time, that difference should come to be less an impediment than a reminder of the pressing issues faced by all systems attempting to do more with less. Technology assessment's strength lies in its perspective being not simply an echo of the general trend to view medical science as a panacea, conferring huge amounts of cost free benefits.

Technology assessment, however, has entered the arena at a time of general questioning of technology's beneficence. As we taste the technological fruits of human genome sequencing, technology assessment will have no choice but to give increasingly central consideration to the ethical, social, and political implications of manipulating the human genome. It is critical that increasingly important considerations of ethics of care are not tossed aside out of a misguided fascination with molecular medicine and the elusive glimpses of meaning discerned by some in DNA sequences. Evaluating technologies cannot help but create a stance more cautious and, I would argue, more insightful and meaningful, with respect to technological innovation.

The paradigm of technology assessment

Can a paradigm for technology assessment be elucidated and what are its implications for both the accumulation of scientific evidence and the provision of health services? I shall begin by considering the ontological, espistemological, and methodological facets of the paradigm and then turn to its consequences.

Technology assessment's deep roots in science suggest that its ontological outlook is predominantly scientific. This is neither

15

good nor bad; it simply reflects that the process to date has been led largely by scientifically oriented people. The drive to uncover the "facts" about such matters as efficacy, effectiveness, and efficiency is at heart reasonable and considering the many lucunae in our knowledge, absolutely essential.

Despite a scientific foundation, and recalling the metaphor of the tree rooted in science, epistemologically and in its methods technology assessment carves out a unique paradigm of its own. The bridge metaphor calls to mind the dynamic and shifting nature of technology assessment—that some questions are predominantly matters of scientific inquiry whereas others are closer to the hermeneutic or interpretive mode of policy making.

The technology assessment framework thus creates spaces for both poles and more importantly, a continuum between them. As I suggested earlier, the future of this framework will probably include increasingly prominent considerations of ethical and philosophical issues, not as a repudiation of the science but in keeping with the bridging notion of technology assessment, providing a means for people as individuals or collectively through policy making to grapple with and delineate the uncertainty arising from genetic markers for diagnosis and prognosis.

The use of methods lies at the heart of technology assessment. Those from the scientific perspective are undoubtedly well known—the randomised controlled trial, the meta-analysis, and other such predominantly quantitive methods. Increasingly, however, qualitative and ethnographic methods are likely to become valuable for technology assessment, particularly when confronting uncertainty and individual approaches to information about risks of future events.

The particular choice of methods is not merely random but should be driven by the policy needs of each decision's particular context. For example, while a randomised controlled trial often provides very precise measures of effect of a drug or intervention, policy decisions must often include factors such as economic costs. As a result, various approaches to linking costs and effects and sensitivity analyses contribute critically to technology assessment.

In short, what is specific and paradigmatic about the methods of technology assessment is not any one approach to investigation in particular but the manner in which technology assessment draws on data from a wide variety of methods. Establishing an interdisciplinary sensibility before considering any of the data is a critical feature of technology assessment.

Any paradigm of technology assessment requires local flavour to translate into a viable activity, but I believe that certain general principles should and must guide the work of technology assessment. I suggest that we situate technology assessment within a framework of responsible stewardship of resources. In most of the world, collectively financed health care systems exist and responsible stewardship is both a product of and supportive of current concerns about ever increasing health care expenditures. Technology assessment, when effective, should hasten the elimination of more wasteful health care technology spending in favour of additional investment in effective technologies or, at the very least, slowing cost growth.

In health care systems built primarily on market based, private sector financing, notably that of the United States, the notion of responsible stewardship is no less applicable. What is fundamentally different, however, is the framework within which resources are managed, exchanging the fiscal health of the collective for the corporate health of the firm, be it an insurer or a service provider. The consequences of eliminating wasteful use in these settings are similar too in that resources are freed. Rather than flowing into deficit or taxation reduction or service expansion, benefits typically accrue to corporate entities.

Considering publicly financed health services available to those in need not in proportion to their ability to pay but, even if only acutely, in proportion to their need, there are equity goals that are advanced through health services, even if only at a rudimentary level. The key battles in the war on mortality—providing safe drinking water and secure sanitation—are still being fought in many countries, but victory is felt by all in terms of halting the spread of communicable disease.

More universally, enhancing information access as technology assessment activities increasingly draw on multiple often contending perspectives levels playing fields in health care decision making. Ideally, this would also have a democratising tendency as access to information broadens.

Furthermore, an additional equity opportunity, linked to responsible stewardship, should arise from the shifting of decisions about service provision from a partisan political realm to a more technical one. Resource constraints may well have hastened this shift, but it seems safe to say that the day is past when a government minister would dispense health care facilities like

17

sweets to children. Voters across the developed world are increasingly suspicious of government promises to spend money, and governments have found methods other than hospital building to win votes. The result is an opening for technical input to decision making about health services, input that cannot be simply dumping journal articles into a policy process but which requires the syntheses and dissemination strategies that mark technology assessment. Though the movement from a political to technical realm may seem counterdemocratic, it seems far more equitable to consider the distribution of acute care hospitals across several areas and select institutions for closure or locations for new ones with some sense of determinants of service use rather than relying on the map of electoral boundaries as a guide to policy making.

The paradigm I propose is thus consistent with responsible stewardship and, to varying degrees, advancing equity. We may argue about the speed of these transformations but I believe that technology assessment cannot truly flourish without them.

Conclusion

I began by developing a series of metaphors with a view to illuminating the paradigm basis of technology assessment. As the objects of inquiry become more complex and involve increasingly conflictual perspectives, the form and methods of technology assessment will be required to accommodate these changes. The future lies in an interdisciplinary, equity advancing approach to making policy about health services. Thinking about that future now will position those who assess technologies and those who use technologies to negotiate the uncertain waters ahead.

I am grateful to Ms H Gelband, Drs R Landry and G Pineau, and Messrs R Jacob, J-M Lance, and G Tombs, for providing comments on an earlier draft, to my students for many lively discussions we had on this topic, and to Dr M J Hodge and Ms A Collins for their assistance in the preparation of the manuscript.

3 Economic evaluation and clinical practice

BENGT JÖNSSON

Economic evaluation and clinical practice raises four different questions:
- What is economic evaluation?
- Why is it relevant for clinical practice?
- What is the scientific standard of economic evaluations?
- What are the incentives for using economic evaluations for clinical practice decisions?

Definition of economic evaluation

Economic evaluation is about allocation of resources. An economic evaluation is a comparison of alternative health care programmes in terms of their cost and consequences or outcome. A true economic evaluation must contain all three elements—alternatives, costs, and outcome. One alternative can be to do nothing. The reason that we undertake economic evaluations is that resources are scarce. It has increasingly been accepted also that the resources available for improving health are limited, although a lot of the rhetoric around allocation of resources in health care still centres around absolute rather than relative criteria—for example, that a certain treatment must be undertaken, regardless of costs and expected outcome. When resources are scarce, choices must be made between competing claims on the resources. These choices are unavoidable. If resources are used for one treatment or patient the same resources cannot be used for another. There is an opportunity cost; the value of the resources in best alternative use.

19

Economic evaluation is about efficiency. Resources will be allocated to different activities and programmes with or without economic evaluations. These should be seen as a tool that can be used to assist decision making to make the best possible use of the available resources. Economic evaluation is not the same as as cost cutting, but it must be recognised that health care expenditures have an opportunity cost. Economic evaluations are relevant regardless of the level of health care expenditure.

Let me make a comment on the relation between the concepts "disease management" and "economic evaluation". Disease management was defined by Sir Richard Sykes as "delivering quality outcome at lowest possible costs". There may be other definitions, but I think this is typical. As both are about costs and outcome you may conclude that disease management and economic evaluation are the same thing. To be a true economic evaluation, however, disease management must firstly, include an explicit discussion of the alternatives; secondly, include an assessment of costs and outcome of variations in the size of the alternative programmes, what economists call marginal analysis; and, thirdly, include an outcome measure that allows relevant comparisons of cost effectiveness.

Why is economic evaluation relevant for clinical practice?

Economic evaluation aims at assisting decision makers to make policy decisions in health care. The major reason why economic evaluation is relevant for clinical practice is that most decisions about allocation of resources in health care are done in clinical practice by the medical professions.

Every physician knows that this is true, but you will often hear two objections. The first is that the politicians and the administrators must take responsibility for priority setting and resource allocation in health care. Politicians and administrators are responsible for decisions about the total amount of resources that is spent for health care and the overall allocation of resources between different types of services. However important these decisions are, they can give only the general framework for allocation of resources in health care. Economic evaluations are obviously useful for assisting these policy decisions as well, but here I will focus on their role for clinical practice.

The second objection is that it is unethical to take costs into account when making decisions about individual patients. Dealing with this issue can lead to an interesting but complicated philosophical discussion about different ethical principles. The distinction I would like to make is between policy decisions and individual patient decisions. Economic evaluations, like technology assessment in general, should be used to deal with policy decisions. That means that they should be used not to discriminate between named patients but for deciding on the criteria that should be applied to all patients should be treated against. These criteria may be explicitly stated in practice guidelines or they can be implicit "rules of thumb".

Clinical practice cannot be practised without criteria. An efficient clinical practice cannot be achieved without defining the appropriate criteria for efficiency. Economic evaluation is a tool for assessing and defining those criteria. But it is not the same as the criteria or the decision itself.

Examples of the importance of clinical decisions for resource allocation

Hypertension and treatment of peptic ulcer disease can serve as examples on the need for economic evaluation in clinical practice. The cost effectiveness of treating hypertension involves two important economic issues: which patients should be treated (the cut off point) and which treatment should be given. The cost effectiveness is related to the risk of stroke and coronary heart disease. This means the cost effectiveness is dependent not only on the level of blood pressure but also on the patient's age and other risk factors.[1] Drugs differ in prices, and patients differ in terms of their response and side effects to different drugs. Economic evaluations can be useful for establishing treatment guidelines, but it is in clinical practice that the efficient use of resources for hypertension are determined. Therefore, clinical practice must be based on an understanding of economic evaluations.

Medical science has produced an increasing number of opportunities for intervention in patients with peptic ulcer disease, antacids, H_2-blockers, proton pump inhibitors, gastroscopy, and laparoscopic vagotomy. The latest treatments are based on the discovery of the role of *Helicobacter pylori* in the development of the disease.[2] The selection of the optimal treatment strategy with all these possible combinations of intervention is a very complicated task. Economic evaluation is part of what is needed for a rational allocation of resources. But unless the clinical

21

practitioner understands the implications of these studies for his or her patients and acts accordingly, there will be no efficient allocation of resources.

These are just two examples. It is possible to choose nearly any other specialty and make the same arguments. The more alternatives medical science produces the more sophisticated must decision making be to optimise the use of these alternatives. This means that the decision making must be decentralised, but also that those making the decisions have the necessary information to base the decisions on. Technology is never cost effective in itself. It is cost effective for a defined indication (patient) in relation to a defined alternative. Since patients and practices differ, clinicians must know how to use economic evaluations to define rational practice criteria.

Are economic evaluations "scientific"?

This collection of papers is about the scientific basis of health services. If economic evaluations should form the basis for decisions in clinical practice they must fulfil reasonable scientific criteria.

Let us first state up front that economic evaluation includes value judgments. These value judgments are mainly related to the definition of the objectives for the health care system; efficiency is how well different allocations or resources meet the objectives. Economic evaluations cannot be used to settle disputes about different values or objectives. But given a strict definition of objectives the implications for efficient use of resources can be analysed in a scientific way.

In fact there is a set of principles of how to undertake economic evaluations that most economists agree about. These principles are basically the same for health care as for other sectors, but they are expressed differently. It is common to make a distinction between four different forms of economic evaluation in health care.
• Cost minimisation analysis
• Cost effectiveness analysis
• Cost utility analysis
• Cost-benefit analysis.

All forms of economic evaluation take costs into account. They differ in terms of how consequences or outcome are measured and valued. The different forms of studies are complementary rather than substitutes. Which one to use depends on the questions asked. For clinical practice, cost minimisation and cost effectiveness analysis are often sufficient. But in settings where interventions affect both quality of life and survival it may be necessary to undertake a cost utility analysis. If there is a need for a direct comparison between costs and patient preferences (willingness to pay) a cost-benefit analysis may be useful. All forms of economic evaluations are based on the same principles—to look for value in relation to costs—but if more general comparisons are needed more assumptions must be made to produce the relevant outcome measures.[3]

The general agreement on the basic principles does not prevent health economists vigorously debating those topics where there is disagreement. I cannot see any difference in this than that we can observe in the medical community. Also in economic evaluation we see great variations in practice patterns. There are good studies and there are bad studies. This will always be the case. The key question is how we can improve on the present situation.

One reason for the fact that we see so many "questionable" economic evaluations is that the general principles for such studies are insufficiently understood by those who undertake the evaluations. In most cases these studies are undertaken by clinicians as an add on to a clinical investigation. In the same way we can see studies by economists that suffer from an incorrect definition of the clinical problem. It is an important step forward that clinicians and health economists increasingly work together in undertaking these studies. This work must start as early as possible and not when the clinical trial is already completed. The employment of health economists within the pharmaceutical industries, which sponsor most clinical trials, is a sign that the importance of this is recognised. The most common criticism of economic evaluation, however, relates to the data used in the study. Economic evaluations are based on three types of data: clinical, epidemiological, and economic.

Surprisingly enough, the criticisms seldom focus on the economic data, practice patterns, costs, etc, but on the clinical and epidemiological data that are needed to define the alternatives studied. Economic evaluations are data hungry. They also reveal the shortcomings of clinical and epidemiological studies. A lesson I have learned is that "a clinical study is never so bad as when you try to use it for an economic evaluation". When listening to all the objections to a clinical study used in an economic evaluation I often have to ask: "If the study is that bad, how can you use it as a basis for clinical decisions"? It is no guarantee that the study is published in a reputable medical journal.

The same with epidemiology. Most clinical studies use surrogate end points of different types, such as blood pressure, lipid levels, bone mineral density, intraocular pressure, or time to progression. To undertake an economic evaluation you must model out the likely outcome of the treatment in a way that can be understood and interpreted. Often the situation is that the evidence of a relation between surrogate end points and relevant outcome variables is weak or even non-existent.

One of the great contributions of economic evaluation to clinical practice is that it puts pressure on those who undertake clinical and epidemiological studies to do these in a way that is more relevant for clinical practice. In fact, the questions the health economist asks are often more relevant for clinical practice decisions than the "scientific" questions asked by the investigators.

The need for guidelines

One question related to economic evaluations that have gained a lot of attention is the fact that the sponsors of different technologies, for example a pharmaceutical firm, have a vested interest in the conclusions from a study. Guidelines for economic evaluations have been suggested as the solution to this problem. I am sceptical of both the "problem" and its "solution".

Guidelines can be useful as a process, as a way of educating and informing about the principles of economic evaluations, but obviously do not change the fact that buyers and sellers in a market have different interests and information. The fact that buyers and sellers have different information is a well known problem in a number of markets, obvious examples are the financial and property markets. Standards for accounting can help to make the market more transparent and reduce transaction costs but are neither necessary nor sufficient. Buyers can undertake their own evaluations and if they lack time or competence they can buy the services from "brokers" in the market.

The scientific journals are the most important brokers for scientific information. It is encouraging to note that some scientific journals, for example *BMJ*, are taking steps to improve the review process for economic evaluations. Publication and open discussion is the best guarantee, actually the only guarantee, for a sound scientific basis for economic evaluations.

What are the incentives for using economic evaluations in clinical practice?

The major incentive for clinicians to use economic evaluations to guide their clinical decisions is the ethical principle to serve the patients and society in the best possible way. We can identify at least three different situations, however, when this may not be enough to produce an efficient allocation of resources.

The first is when it is unclear who the patients are. It is important that clinical decisions take into account not only the patients under treatment but also potential patients, for example on a waiting list. Decisions about referrals for specialist investigations, admission to hospital, length of hospital stay, choice of treatment, etc, must take into account that both actual and potential patients count. A population based mechanism for the allocation of resources may help to give the proper incentives for these decisions.

The second is when the relevant costs are so spread in time or space that they cannot be controlled by the clinician; they fall outside his or her budget. An economic evaluation should take a social perspective. All costs, whenever or wherever they occur, should be taken into account. But in reality the health care system is made up of a myriad of budgets, and a clinical decision may increase the cost in one budget while reducing the cost within another. For example, an increase in drug expenditures could reduce hospital expenditures, perhaps several years later. A special problem is when the benefits come in terms of reduced indirect costs that benefit employers or the tax payers in general. If they are ignored they will lead to an inefficient allocation of resources. There is no simple solution to this problem, but the struggle towards global budgets, for example the HMO model in private insurance systems, and a separation of purchasers and providers in public health care systems is a step towards a more comprehensive view of costs. Economic evaluations may be of great value to point to the problems that still exist; they take a societal perspective but at the same time they can look into who gets the benefits and who carries the costs (differentiation of the perspective of the analysis). The fact that costs and benefits fall on different budgets is as much an argument for economic evaluation as against it.

The third setting is when clinical decision makers are faced with economic incentives that are contrary to what is cost effective medical practice. Hospitals that are paid per day are known to have long lengths of stay. If you are trying to introduce laparoscopic surgery in such a system, there is obviously a problem. To pay for the more expensive procedure, at least in the short run, the patients have to stay even longer. Systems that pay the doctor a fee per visit are known to have many visits. A new drug that reduces the need for monitoring and control may never produce the potential savings because it is contrary to the economic interests of the doctor.

The methods we use to pay doctors and hospitals provide strong incentives for clinical behaviour, both in private and public health care systems. You sometimes listen to debates about the pros and cons of introducing economic incentives in the health care system. But the choice is not to introduce them; they are already there. The choice is to change them. Cataract surgery can provide an example. When hospital departments are given budgets to undertake cataract surgery you may have a reduction in length of stay when technology improves but you will never get a switch to outpatient surgery. You will probably also have long waiting lists, if this can be used as an indicator for need for an increased budget. If you pay per procedure you will soon see that the hospital will change to outpatient surgery. And waiting lists will disappear and the number of patients treated will increase. Then you will get another problem; how to determine the optimal number of treated patients? This will not be solved with the new payment system, but it allows you to focus on the different measures that can be undertaken to address this issue, instead of spending your management resources changing the practice to a more cost effective method of treatment.

Conclusion

Economic evaluations are increasingly relevant for clinical practice. The progress of medical science produces new opportunities for intervention which force patients and health policy makers to make choices. Due to the uncertainty involved in medical decision making and the heterogeneity of patients, most of these choices have to be made in clinical practice. Political and administrative decision making can give only the overall priorities.

There is a set of well established principles for economic evaluation in health care, and we can look forward to further development in methodology. There will, however, always be unsettled controversies and opportunities for further improvements. In this respect health economics does not differ from other sciences.

In terms of practical application progress has been made, but there is still a long way to go. Accounting systems in health care are still developing, and data on costs that are relevant for clinical decision making are still very limited. Economic evaluations must be based on accurate clinical and epidemiological data. So far clinical trials and epidemiological studies have rarely been planned with the purpose to be used to study questions about allocation of resources. This is gradually changing, but the process is slow and it is understandable that clinical researchers and epidemiologists prefer to proceed with "business as usual". But studying the economic issues will not only complicate the clinical studies, it will also make them more relevant for health policy decisions. One of the important contributions of health economics and health technology assessment in general is to focus studies on aspects that are of interest for society at large, for those who use and pay for the health services.

My personal experience is that clinical practitioners are not only interested in efficiency and economic evaluations, they are also prepared to take on this new and difficult project. The reason for this is, I think, that they find it relevant, important, and challenging. And, if they are not doing it, someone else will do it for them. It is important to emphasise that it is knowledge about health economics and economic evaluations that is needed in the health services not necessarily more health economists.

The competence in health economics and economic evaluation is increasing in the health services, but it is lagging behind the building up of this competence in the health technology industries, the pharmaceutical industry in particular. In the longer run a more balanced situation must and will occur because information needs both a sender and receiver to be useful. Economic evaluations undertaken by the industry, ideally in cooperation with the potential users, can be of great value for clinical practice in the future in the same way as safety and effectiveness studies have been for a long time. Economic evaluations also offer an opportunity to assess the incentives that are given to the industry to develop new technologies. If the industry is given the incentive to develop cost effective technologies it will be easier to implement these in clinical practice and the waste of resources will be reduced. If clinical practice gives the wrong incentives the wrong technologies will be developed.

Economic evaluation of clinical practice is an important factor for both short term and long term efficiency in the allocation of scarce health care resources for the benefit of patients and payers.

1 Jönsson BG. Cost-benefit of treating hypertension. *Journal of Hypertension* 1994; **12**(suppl 10): S65–S70.

2 Unge P, Jönsson B, Stålhammar N-O. The cost effectiveness of helicobacter pylori eradication versus maintenance and episodic treatment in duodenal ulcer patients in Sweden. *Pharmaco Economics* 1995; **8**(5): 410–27.

3 Johannesson M, Jönsson B, Karlsson G. Outcome measurement in economic evaluation. Stockholm: Stockholm School of Economics, Mimeo.

4 Impact of management on outcomes

LIAM J DONALDSON

The work of a modern health service is directed towards five broad aims:

- To improve the health of the population
- To produce better quality of care for patients
- To enhance the quality of life (particularly of people with long term needs)
- To generate greater efficiency
- To ensure greater equity in health and in the care provided.[1]

In most countries, the health care system is such that these aims are dealt with through a large number of organisations and a huge and diverse workforce. A health service seeking to achieve optimum outcomes through its work must acknowledge the difficulty in understanding how beneficial change can be secured in such a complex environment through planned intervention.

The idea that health services will be more effective if staff with purely managerial responsibilities are employed is a relatively recent one. The emergence of health care management seems to have been prompted by several influences. Firstly, it is perceived that effective cost containment will not be achieved without drawing health care professionals into a framework of accountability. Secondly, there is a belief that the benefits of modern management strategies demonstrated in the business sector could and should apply equally to health care organisations, such as hospitals. Thirdly, those who fund health care (whether governmental or otherwise) require clearer accountability for performance given the large sums of money they invest. Fourthly, the processes and transactions created by the system of health care itself, such as contracting and costing, will be better carried out by professional managers, without needlessly diverting clinicians' time. Fifthly, there are benefits in having senior people within an organisation who are able to view services from a lay or patient perspective, rather than a purely professional one.

The impact of management within a health service should be judged principally by the extent to which it enables more people to experience better health outcomes within the total funds available. In turn, this depends on the achievement of two goals: creating the right environment for the delivery of patient services (including staff and facilities) and ensuring that the professionals who actually diagnose and treat patients do so more effectively.

Better outcomes through better health care

Some would say that outcome is the most important aspect of the quality of care provided to patients. Outcome is the third component of Donabedian's durable and highly respected conceptualisation of health care quality—structure (for example, hospitals, equipment, personnel, resources), process (what is done for and to patients and how well), and outcome (the effects of care).[2] Despite the increasing emphasis placed on outcomes in professional debates about the correct focus in defining quality of care[3] and despite the longstanding existence of frameworks for describing outcomes[4] there is little evidence of day to day availability or use of outcome data in professional practice or in health service management. The absence of comprehensive and validated data on health outcome has not deterred policy makers and managers in some health care systems from releasing comparative data on hospital mortality directly to the public in the belief that this use of outcome data is an important vehicle for improving performance.[5] This "report card" approach is likely to become much more common despite methodological criticisms[6] so that hospitals, increasingly, will have to take outcomes seriously.

It is difficult to see how a health care organisation can align its management strategies, its work, and its staff towards the achievement of particular outcomes when there is such a paucity of relevant data through which to assess progress. Nevertheless, there is mounting evidence that the outcome of clinical care is both variable and, in many cases, capable of improvement.[7] This and other concerns about the appropriateness and effectiveness of medical care have produced, in the 1990s, a more widespread commitment towards professionally led quality improvement activities.

Central to this new interest in a more systematic approach to achieving improved outcomes of clinical care has been the emergence of a new philosophy of evidence based medical practice (described elsewhere in this book). This emphasis, described as a "paradigm shift",[8] has not only sought to bring a new and more scientifically based rigour to day to day clinical decision making but also to evaluate specific mechanisms for quality improvement (such as consensus conferences, guidelines, and protocols) to decide which approaches are effective before they are deployed.[9] [10] Where these changes have been introduced they have required health care professionals to develop new skills, including the ability to access electronic databases and undertake critical appraisal of the scientific literature. Continuing medical education, one route to enhancing such skills, is itself being subjected to a review of effectiveness.[11]

The capacity of management to influence the outcome of care received by patients is largely a feature of the range of actions that management can take to enable doctors and other health care professionals to make better decisions and interventions and to ensure that they make best use of the opportunity.

Better health care through better management

Classic 19th century theories of management were highly hierarchical and saw organisations as analogous to an armed force with foot soldiers (the workers) whose task was to carry out the instructions of the officers (managers) whose task was to command. Henri Fayol thus described the components of management as being to forecast, plan, organise, command, coordinate, and control.[12] More recent theories of the managerial function have recognised that simple "command and control" models neither reflect the complexity of the modern working environment nor do they motivate staff properly. For example, in the early 1970s Mintzberg described management as having three broad roles: interpersonal (figurehead, leader, liaison); informational (monitor, disseminator, spokesperson); and decisional (entrepreneur, disturbance handler, resource allocator, negotiator).[13]

The increasing complexity and globalisation of product markets and financial markets, the pace of technological change, and the growing sophistication of consumers have created a competitive pressure that is probably without precedent. The management structures of the 1970s are widely seen to have been inadequate in a rapidly changing environment. Modern management thinking has therefore focused on the goal of more flexible organisations that are more adaptable to change and have fewer levels of formal hierarchy and loose boundaries among functions.[14] Where Mintzberg reserved the decisional functions within the organisation to management, more recent analysts see it as essential that these functions be distributed as widely as possible to achieve the necessary adaptability, responsiveness, and efficiency in the organisation as a whole.[14 15]

Earlier notions of managing hospitals floundered on the problem of preserving the autonomy which is enshrined within professions such as medicine and nursing.[16] Traditionally, too few health service managers have been able to cope with the complexity and subtlety of leading a highly skilled and educated professional workforce and avoiding the polarised approaches of either being insufficiently willing to challenge or inappropriately autocratic.[17] Ironically, during the period in which health services became aware of the apparent benefits of introducing managerial skill, business management thinking shifted significantly away from lingering notions of "command and control" to concepts based on teamwork and empowerment. This framework is much more in accord with the professional traditions of clinicians. In addition, the central task of management today is perceived as being to guide and accomplish the change from inherited organisational structures to the "learning organisation".[18] It is argued that this task is essentially the same across all kinds of organisations despite "differences in detail" between sectors and organisations.[14] In many health care systems today accountability for performance and use of funds rests with full time managers. Those leading health care organisations are increasingly seeking to find new ways to produce improved performance in an environment where there is pressure from demographic trends, rapid technological advance, growing consumer expectation, and limited budgets.

Managing outcomes

The approach to managing outcomes in health care rests on an understanding of what actions can be taken to shape and influence professional behaviour effectively as well as on the choice of appropriate strategies to lead and motivate staff in organisations. At the heart of action to enable health care professionals to achieve improved outcome is the question of how to ensure a greater uptake of those research findings that have implications for better practice. This does not happen sufficiently well at present, as Eddy has observed "the profession has placed value on developing the basic of science of medicine; it has not emphasised the process by which the science is translated into practice".[19] The whole topic of effectiveness in the dissemination and utilisation of the results of research has been widely studied and reviewed.[20] Six strategies have been identified by Backer through analysis of relevant studies.[21]

Critical strategies for knowledge utilisation[21]

- Interpersonal contact

- Planning and conceptual foresight

- Outside consultation on the change process

- User orientated transformation of information

- Individual and organisational championship

- Potential user involvement

Rogers has studied the process of diffusion of innovations for more than 30 years and has shown that four main elements are identifiable in any diffusion research study or programme: the innovation itself, the communication channels involved, the period of time, and the social system concerned.[22] An innovation is an idea that is seen to be new by an individual or organisation. Thus the definition can be extended to a new practice or procedure. Adoption is influenced by a complex range of factors including the perceived attributes of the innovation (relative advantage, compatibility with existing beliefs, complexity, trialability, and observability), whether communication is via mass media or face to face, and the social structure of the organisation (particularly opinion leadership and networks).[22]

The rate of adoption over time almost always follows an S shaped curve (figure 4.1) starting with a relatively small number of innovators (who adopt the new practice through reading widely or hearing of it through their extensive networks). Then it is taken up by so called "early adopters". This is the group of opinion leaders. Its members are most influential in changing the behaviour of the majority. Diffusion is a social process. Even if they are aware of the evidence most people in an organisation will adopt an innovation, a new practice, or a different behaviour largely because of local experience and discussion with their immediate peers. A wide range of specific approaches has been shown to influence professional behaviour in planned interventions.

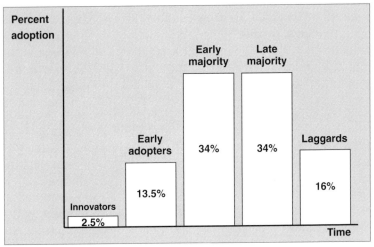

Figure 4.1 Sequence of adoption of innovations in a social system (adapted from Rogers[22]).

Evidence from this specialty is of direct relevance to health care management, which is seeking to produce change in professional behaviour to improve outcomes of care. The task of integrating such an approach into an overall management strategy, however, is immensely complex. There is little evidence that the lessons of diffusion and utilisation research are being operationalised (say) in the management of hospitals. Nevertheless, it is important that health care management does deal with these concepts, particularly in understanding the way in which local professional

---

Interventions that have been used to improve the performance of health care professionals and evaluated by trials[23]

- Educational materials

- Conferences

- Outreach visits

- Local opinion leaders

- Patient mediated interventions

- Audit and feedback

- Reminders

- Marketing

- Multifaceted interventions

- Local consensus processes

---

networks can be effectively used and in recognising the role of opinion formers in connecting external knowledge and local context.[24]

Consideration of how to provide the best environment for modern health care to operate begins conventionally with management giving attention to physical issues such as buildings and equipment. Ensuring that health care professionals have access to (and know how to use) the "external knowledge" is likely to be the greatest challenge over the next decade. As Sisk has put it: "the ultimate purpose of changing practice to conform to best evidence is to improve health outcomes and to provide care more efficiently and more equitably".[25] Thus, one of management's tasks in promoting evidence based medicine with the health care organisation is to provide, for its doctors and other professional staff, information resources to support their work. One particular

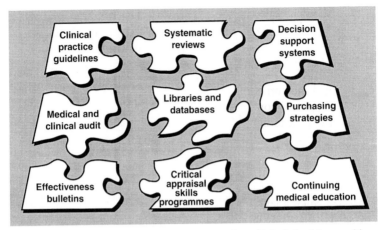

Figure 4.2 Various approaches to improving clinical decision making. How does everything fit together?

challenge is to identify and integrate all the different approaches to improving the quality of clinical decision making (see figure 4.2). By working with librarians, information technologists, and communications experts the leader of a health care organisation can ensure that the professional staff have access to general and specialised electronic databases, to relevant journals and systematic reviews of the literature, and to practice guidelines. Such front line staff must also be equipped with key skills such as accessing and critically appraising the literature.[26 27]

In addition to empowering staff to improve the outcomes of care by providing them with infrastructure, resources, and training there are other aspects to creating an effective organisational environment. This does not simply mean designing a structure. Much more important and fruitful areas of definition include the style of the organisation and its values. Creating an effective organisation that will then lead to a more effective workforce that will in turn achieve improved outcomes has been a corporate obsession during the 1980s and 1990s. In the business sector organisational transformation has taken a variety of different forms[28]: total quality management, re-engineering, right sizing, restructuring, and cultural change. Other approaches based on improving systems and processes have also been influential.[18]

Most evaluations of these strategies have been based on qualitative techniques such as case studies (though measures of company performance can also be used to assess impact). Some of these concepts, either because they have had success in the corporate world or because they have such a high face validity, have been widely promoted in the health services field. Foremost among them is total quality management, also called continuous quality improvement.[29] [30] Such approaches introduce an organisational philosophy based on concepts of leadership, empowerment of staff, team work, prevention (rather than correction) of adverse outcome, and a strong customer focus. Formal evaluations are increasingly common, though there are problems with defining the "intervention" and the generalisability of the programmes. For example, a study of 584 companies (mainly non-health sector) found a total of 945 programmes each designed by different experts.[31] Such a lack of standardisation is unlikely to be different in health care, where interest in other organisational transformation methods such as process re-engineering is growing. Health care managers will increasingly take their lead from models of change in other sectors particularly as many now seek to attend Masters of Business Administration (MBA) programmes, where multidisciplinary teaching is common. The introduction of strategies in health care based on organisational development and restructuring will need careful evaluation because it cannot be assumed that their inherent attractiveness will necessarily lead to demonstrably improved outcomes of care.

Finally, in ensuring good performance of their organisations managers need oversight of clinical areas to ensure that their corporate goals are delivered. This balancing of clinical, managerial, and organisational performance and accountability is one of the most contentious aspects of management's role. It has been seen by doctors as a threat to their professionalism.[32] The issue has generated particular controversy in the United States, where it is attributed to the growth of managed care. In late 1994 the *New York Times*, commenting on the evolution of the United States health care system towards managed care through health maintenance organisations (in which a predetermined payment replaces fees for individual services), noted that three quarters of doctors had agreed contracts that accepted oversight of their medical decisions in some way.[33] There have been calls for salaried physicians to work for self regulated, physician managed organisations and not be direct employees of business corporations.[34]

In many health care systems of the world deciding an approach to management is not simply a task for the individual health care organisation concerned. Rather, the design of the health care system itself is of fundamental importance. The scale of health care reform in many countries of the world, including Britain, other European countries, and the United States, means that the management of individual organisations and the professional staff within them must be seen in the wider context of the health care system as many managerial strategies will be set on this basis. As is becoming evident in the NHS, however, new mechanisms (such as contracting) open to managers within the system of care will increasingly be used to deal with issues of quality of care, including improving its outcome.[35]

Conclusions

A major and widely acknowledged weakness of most health care systems is their inability to produce valid and comprehensive measures of the outcome of the care provided. While it must be remembered that patient care accounts for only the minority of health outcomes (the population health perspective[36]), quality of health care will increasingly be judged on data on outcome of patient care. Already the public have access to such information to enable them to compare hospital performance, despite cynicism about its validity. Outcome is largely determined by the actions of health care professionals so that the impact of management on outcome must be judged mainly on managers' ability to get the best out of doctors, nurses, and other care groups. Health care

---

The hallmark of the new organisation[37]

- Radical decentralisation

- Intense interdependence

- Demanding expectations

- Transparent performance standards

- Distributed leadership

- Boundary busting

- Networking and reciprocity

---

management strategies must take account of the evidence on how best to influence professionals' behaviour, they must seek to enhance the uptake of research findings into everyday practice (particularly through providing infrastructure and an environment for carrying out evidence based health care), they must also seek to adopt the organisational models and philosophies from other sectors which have been shown to be beneficial (figure 4.3). The radical shift away from traditional organisational structures and ways of working whose principles are being espoused in other

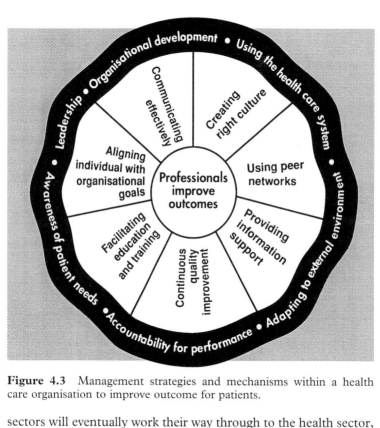

Figure 4.3 Management strategies and mechanisms within a health care organisation to improve outcome for patients.

sectors will eventually work their way through to the health sector, where they will be advocated. Ways of working based on information sharing, team learning, and networking have much in common with the traditions of the professions. These approaches could provide the flexibility to allow health care managers to lead effectively without producing the conflict which has arisen in the past from perceived challenge to professional autonomy.

1 Donaldson RJ, Donaldson LJ. *Essential public health medicine*. London: Kluwer, 1993: 194–5.

2 Donabedian A. Evaluating the quality of medical care. *Milbank Memorial Fund Quarterly* 1966; **44** suppl: 166–206.

3 Irvine D, Donaldson LJ. Quality and standards in health care. *Proceedings of the Royal Society of Edinburgh* 1993; **101B**: 1–30.

4 Lohr KN. Outcome measurement: concepts and questions. *Inquiry* 1988; **25**: 37–50.

5 *New York Times* 1986 March 12.

6 Green JU, Wintfeld N. Report cards on cardiac surgeons: assessing New York State's approach. *N Engl J Med* 1995; **332**: 1229–32.

7 McPherson K. How should health policy be modified by the evidence of medical practice variations? In: Marinker M, ed, *Controversies in healthcare policies*. London: BMJ Publishing Group, 1994: 57–74.

8 Evidence-based Medicine Working Group. Evidence-based medicine: a new approach to teaching the practice of medicine. *JAMA* 1992; **268**: 2420–5.

9 Kanouse DE, Winkler JD, Kosecoff J, *et al*. *Changing medical practice through technology assessment: an evaluation of the NIH consensus development program*. Santa Monica: RAND Corporation, 1989.

10 *Implementing clinical practice guidelines*. Leeds: University of Leeds, 1994. (Effective Healthcare Bulletin No. 8.)

11 Davis DA, Thompson MA, Oxman AD, *et al*. Evidence for the effectiveness of CME: a review of 50 randomised controlled trials. *JAMA* 1992; **268**: 1111–7.

12 Fayol H. *General and industrial management*. London: Pitman, 1949.

13 Mintzberg H. *The nature of managerial work*. New York: Harper Row, 1973.

14 Moss Kanter R, Stein BA, Jick TD. *The challenge of organisational change*. New York: Free Press, 1992: 3.

15 Pascale RT. *Managing on the edge*. London: Viking, 1990.

16 Freidson EI. *Profession of medicine*. New York: Dodd, Mead, 1970.

17 Donaldson LJ. Conflict, power, negotiation. *BMJ* 1995; **310**: 104–7.

18 Senge PM. *The fifth discipline: the art and practise of the learning organisation*. London: Century Business, 1992.

19 Eddy DM. Clinical policies and the quality of clinical practice. *N Engl J Med* 1982; **307**: 343–7.

20 Backer TE. Knowledge utilisation: the third wave. *Knowledge: Creation, Diffusion, Utilisation* 1991; **12**: 225–40.

21 Backer TE. *Utilisation: the challenge of transferring innovation in rehabilitation and special education*. Washington DC: DATA Institute, 1986.

22 Rogers EM. *Diffusion of innovations*. 4th ed. New York: Free Press, 1995.

23 Oxman AD. *No magic bullets: a systematic review of 102 trials of interventions to help health care professionals deliver services more effectively and efficiently*. London: North Thames Regional Health Authority, 1984.

24 Greer AL. The shape of resistance, the shapers of change. *Jt Comm J Qual Improv* 1995; **21**: 328–32.

25 Sisk JE. Promises and hazards of strategies to implement change. *Jt Comm J Qual Improv* 1995; **21**: 357–60.

26 Oxman AD, Sackett DL, Guyatt GH. Users' guide to the medical literature. How to get started. *JAMA* 1993; **270**: 2093–5.

27 Bennett KJ, Sackett DL, Haynes RB, *et al*. A controlled trial of teaching critical appraisal of the clinical literature to medical students. *JAMA* 1987; **257**: 2451–4.

28 Kolter JP. Leading change: why transformation efforts fail. *Harvard Business Review* 1995; March–April: 59–67.

29 Deming WE. *Out of the crisis*. Cambridge: Cambridge University Press, 1986.

30 Berwick DM. Continuous improvement as an ideal in health care. *N Engl J Med* 1989; **320**: 53–6.

31 The International Quality Study. *Best practices report*. Cleveland, Ohio: American Quality Foundation and Ernst & Young, 1992.
32 Rodwin MA. Conflicts in managed care. *N Engl J Med* 1995; **332**: 604–7.
33 *New York Times* 1994 December 18.
34 Relman AS. Salaried physicians and economic incentives. *N Engl J Med* 1988; **319**: 784.
35 Donaldson LJ. Building quality into contracting and purchasing. *Quality in Health Care* 1994; **3** suppl: 37–40.
36 Wilkinson RG. National mortality rates: the impact of inequality. *Am J Public Health* 1992; **82**: 1082–4.
37 Hastings C. *The new organisation: growing the culture of organisational networking.* Maidenhead: McGraw-Hill, 1993: 3.

5 Advances in genetics: implications for health services and social and ethical issues

SALLY MACINTYRE

Several recent publications have drawn attention to the potential significance for the health services of advances in molecular genetics. In the United Kingdom we can note in particular the report of the Health and Life Sciences panel of the technology foresight exercise,[1] the first and second reports of the Genetics Research Advisory Group,[2][3] and the House of Commons science and technology committee's report *Human genetics: the science and its consequences.*[4]

These reports, and many others, draw attention to two things: the enormous impact that "the new genetics" may have on screening for and prevention and treatment of disease; and the wide range of social and ethical issues which "the new genetics" raise and which need to be given serious consideration, not just by clinicians and geneticists but by society in general.

Awareness of the potentially difficult social and ethical issues raised by advances in genetics has prompted a number of systematic reviews of the subject,[5–9] and 3% of the budget for the human genome initiative in the United States was set aside to study ethical, legal, and social implications of the mapping of the human genome.[7] It is impossible to give a comprehensive summary of these reviews here so I will focus on selected issues that may be particularly important for an evidence based health service, illustrating these mainly but not exclusively with reference to breast cancer and cystic fibrosis.

Social and ethical issues

It is important to emphasise that many of the social and ethical issues often discussed in relation to the new genetics are not really new at all but are similar in principle (and possibly in practice) to those in existing areas of screening, prevention, and treatment.

In the long run, it is hoped, better understanding of gene products and their functions will lead to the rational design of drug therapies and more targeted delivery systems or other treatments such as dietary regimens, which are no different in principle from current therapies. It is argued, for example, that better understanding of the BRCA1 gene and its role in breast cancer might in the long run lead to the development of drugs or dietary regimen that could be used to prevent or treat breast cancer.[10] Such pharmacological or dietary treatments may be little different in principle from treating a diabetic with insulin or recommending a special diet for a newborn detected by screening as having phenylketonuria. Somatic gene therapy for cystic fibrosis, which is currently receiving a lot of research attention, may not differ in principle from organ transplantation in other conditions, both treating the phenotype (but not genotype) with foreign products. Such therapies would be subject to trials of efficacy and long term costs and benefits in the same way as therapies for non-genetic conditions. They thus would not pose problems for an evidence based health service that are any different from those posed by other experimental and expensive procedures such as prophylactic tamoxifen for the prevention of breast cancer in women at high risk of breast cancer because of family history, in vitro fertilisation, or organ transplantation.

Specific problems

In the medium term the main health service applications of the new genetics will be screening for carriers of recessive disorders, prenatal screening and diagnosis for gene mutations that carry disease with a view to termination of pregnancy for affected fetuses, and testing for genetic predisposition for disorders with adult onset. Some ethical and social issues raised by these applications are similarly not specific to genetic conditions, although they may be posed in a particularly acute form by possibilities created by the new genetics or by the enthusiasm of those wishing to see their potential realised.

The ethical principles underlying any screening programme—These include that all relevant scientific evidence should be taken into account, that the condition is an important one, that there should be an effective treatment for it, and that the benefits of screening outweigh the costs.[12] There is no reason in principle why these standards should not be applied to screening for genotype as they are to screening for phenotype (for example, for BRCA1 mutations as compared with mammography for detection of early cancers).

Issues relating to counselling—To be considered are the effectiveness of counselling, the extent to which people understand the information given, the validity of informed consent for screening or treatment, and the extent to which counselling is or should be non-directive. The issues in relation to genetic testing or screening or to any consequent treatment decisions are no different from those raised by many other, non-genetics conditions, such as HIV or Down's syndrome, for which patients may be offered counselling before deciding on diagnosis or treatment.

The circumstances and conditions for which termination of pregnancy is regarded as justified—There is no difference in principle between chromosomal abnormalities such as Down's syndrome or congenital malformations such a neural tube defects and inherited conditions such as cystic fibrosis or Duchenne muscular dystrophy, in the dilemmas they pose for deciding whether or not to terminate a pregnancy. (Although in the future termination of pregnancy may be advocated for carriers of recessive conditions, or for reduction of mutant genotypes in the gene pool.)

Patients' rights—These include the rights of individual patients to have or to refuse consequential information about themselves; their rights to refuse to pass on this information to those who might be affected; the rights of others to this information; and the responsibilities of medical and genetics professionals to maintain or breach confidentiality. These are no different in principle from those relating to communicable diseases such as hepatitis, typhoid, or HIV, which may pose risks to others as well as to the person affected.

The new genetics, however, has tended to refocus attention on some of these issues, for several reasons.

Increased pervasiveness and relevance for larger sectors of the population than previous screening and testing services—In the past many such services were available only for pregnant women or for families who themselves sought genetic advice on the basis of their family history, but now, particularly in relation to carrier status for cystic fibrosis, they are being extended to other populations such as teenagers or people attending general practice for other reasons.[13]

44

Production of greater certainty—Rather than someone simply having a family history of cystic fibrosis or breast cancer it will be possible to test him or her to see whether they have actually inherited the relevant gene mutation. This means for example that siblings who may previously have thought they were all equally at risk can now be separated into those who are and are not at risk.[10]

Current lack of effective treatment—Examples being that the only "treatment" option available for couples identified as both being carriers of cystic fibrosis is prenatal diagnosis and termination of affected fetuses, and for women found to have the BCRA1 gene the only "treatment" options are preventive bilateral mastectomies and oophorectomies or increased frequency of surveillance by mammography; none of these can be regarded as being treatments in the classic sense.

Lifelong implications for patient and family members—For example, if I have a BRCA1 mutation my daughters have a 50-50 chance of inheriting it; if I have cystic fibrosis my mother must be a carrier. The meanings of one's genotype are thus different from those of one's phenotype, both for oneself and for one's kindred.

Questions for health services

These aspects of the new genetics potentially raise a number of questions

Will the greater certainty about inherited susceptibility provided by molecular genetics have different social and health services implications from those arising from general knowledge of family history?

Women already have some notion of a general familial tendency to breast cancer, and this may colour their responses to advice to undertake breast self examination or regular mammography; the question is whether the additional certainty created by genetic tests poses a different situation. Almost immediately after the identification of BRCA1 a woman who had previously decided to undergo a prophlyactic mastectomy on the basis of the family history of breast cancer was tested for the mutation and was found not to have it; she was thus able to cancel her operation.[14] There is some evidence that members of susceptible families already have ideas about who among them is likely to be affected. Two sisters of a 31 year old woman with breast cancer were tested for BRCA1; one was told that she had inherited susceptibility while the other one was told she had not, and both were surprised because they had assumed the susceptibility was the other way round.[10] We do not yet know the consequences of such specific diagnoses of genetic susceptibility for personal identity, family dynamics, health service use, and insurance eligibility, but we do know from studies of Huntington's disease, breast cancer, and familial adenomatous polyposis that people's responses are not always what would have been predicted by those proponents of testing who feel that knowledge of one's genetic make up is of itself a good thing.

What behavioural responses will people have to being assessed as being at high or low risk of disorders, and how effective will any consequent preventive actions be?

It sometimes seems to be assumed that testing for genetic susceptibility to disorders will be beneficial and cost effective for society and health services because people informed that they are at risk will take effective action to lower their risk. There is no empirical evidence, however, to suggest either that people will respond in this way or that their responses would be effective in reducing the risk. There is, for example, no evidence that people informed as teenagers or in adult life that they are carriers of cystic fibrosis will change their marriage or reproductive plans as a result. Even in communities with visibly high rates of recessively inherited disorders and programmes of premarital carrier testing there is little evidence that the testing programme changes people's marriage plans; in Cyprus, for example, engaged couples both found to be carriers of thalassaemia tend to marry anyway and to opt for prenatal diagnosis and abortion of affected fetuses despite the Orthodox church's disapproval of abortion.[15]

The justification for testing for a BRCA1 mutation is that the affected women can take preventive action, but it is not clear, firstly, how many of them will opt for the few actions that are available (mastectomy or frequent surveillance) and, secondly, how effective these actions will be.

The issue of people's responses to genetic risk is crucial when we move from relatively rare conditions to common, multifactorial conditions such as diabetes, hypertension, asthma, coronary heart disease, and several forms of cancer. As has been pointed out in relation to heart disease there are two psychologically plausible responses to being told that one is at genetically high risk: thinking that if heart disease is predetermined, there is no point worrying about smoking, drinking, cholesterol testing, and weight control; or thinking that as one is at risk it is important to modify that risk by being very careful. (Equally, if one is at low risk one may either think that gives licence to smoke, drink, etc, or think it is important to maintain the low risk by careful attention to lifestyle). The problem is that we do not know how many of what sorts of people, in what circumstances, and in relation to what disorders are likely to have which of these responses.[16] If people increasingly come to believe that all diseases are genetically determined they may become more sceptical about the capacity of behavioural or environmental modifications to improve health. If people defined as being at either level of risk tend to follow the first course (no point leading a healthy lifestyle) the overall effect on the nation's health might be adverse.

Should genetic screening be offered even if there is no effective treatment available for the disease in question?

The principle that population screening should not be offered unless there is an effective treatment available and the condition is important and widespread has been accepted in most areas of medical practice and has been reiterated recently by the chief medical officer for England and Wales.[12] The boundaries of what constitutes effective treatment, however, are being stretched by the new possibilities for screening being created by the new genetics. The recent first report of the Genetics Research Advisory Group to the NHS research and development programme, for example, states that: "Overall the principles of genetic screening are similar to issues involved in other fields except with regard to the possibility for intervention. After genetic screening, interventions may include changes in lifestyle or reproductive decisions, as well as medical interventions in the conventional sense".[2]

There are no demonstrably effective treatments that can be offered as a result of screening for carrier status of cystic fibrosis, testing for BCRA1 in affected families, or testing newborn boys for Duchenne muscular dystrophy, but screening and testing for these are already in place in the United Kingdom at least in experimental settings (and in the case of cystic fibrosis, commercially). It is argued that although there may not be effective treatments, there are benefits to be derived from such programmes for individual patients, families, and the public health as a whole. In relation to the screening programme for Duchenne muscular dystrophy in Wales for example, the aims are described as being "to give families reproductive choice in future pregnancies; to enable them to plan for the future with a child with disability; to avoid the experience of prolonged diagnosis; and to identify a presymptomatic cohort who may benefit from future treatments".[17]

There are two issues here. The first is whether or not these benefits are found to be realised; the screening programme might instead have adverse psychological and social consequences, for example some people might argue that "forewarned that your baby will later show signs of muscle wasting, you might suffer years of anxiety to no avail. Perhaps the knowledge could even harm your relationship with your child. You might even feel stigmatised as 'genetically inferior', be pressurised to reveal your genetic status to employers and distant relatives, and find it difficult to get private insurance for your family".[18]

The experimental screening programmes currently in place in the United Kingdom are all being evaluated so evidence should soon become available about their benefits and disbenefits. (Although in the United States it has already been argued that screening for incurable diseases should be avoided because it has no benefits.[19])

The second issue is whether even if these benefits are shown to be produced they count as "effective treatments" in the sense originally meant in discussions of the effectiveness of screening and whether they are the sorts of benefits that a publicly financed health service should fund, given not only the absolute costs of the screening service but also the opportunity costs (money spent on screening for recessively inherited disorders may not in consequence be available for the treatment or prevention of other disorders). The question of whether or not they produce the expected benefits and the specific weighing of the costs and benefits (including psychosocial costs and benefits) is a matter for systematic research and assessment of evidence. The question of whether or not the health service is in the business of producing these specific sorts of benefits is a matter for political and social judgment. Again this is not a totally novel situation; techniques such as cosmetic surgery or in vitro fertilisation may entail medical, nursing, and laboratory professions and may be shown to be beneficial to the people concerned, but we may, nevertheless, not regard them as sufficiently high priority to be provided under a publicly funded health service.

Will there be an increased "geneticisation of society" and if so what will be the health service consequences?

Several of the recent publications have taken the view that the new genetics will have a huge impact on medicine and society and be extremely pervasive.[1][3] Some commentators have been warning for some time that this might lead to the geneticisation of society and of cultural values, with a variety of unfortunate consequences. Geneticisation has been described by one author as "an ongoing process by which differences between individuals are reduced to their DNA codes, with most disorders, behaviours and physiological variations defined, at least in part, as genetic in origin".[20]

I will not here discuss the wider implications of geneticisation, such as social attitudes to behaviour and personal responsibility, but only those relating to evidence based health services. One set of concerns relates to attitudes to abortion and to disability. It has been suggested that the ability to detect handicapping conditions in utero will lead to pressure on parents to abort these pregnancies, stigmatisation and blame for those who do not, and lack of resources for people born with disabilities on the grounds that disability will be seen as avoidable and therefore blameworthy. This fear partly arises from the cost-benefit calculations sometimes made about the effects of screening programmes on birth incidence, which imply that the goal is reduction of birth incidence. A related fear is that health service resources will be increasingly devoted to genetic conditions because of the scientific excitement currently being generated by molecular genetics, to the detriment of non-genetic preventive, therapeutic, or caring strategies or services, and of concerns about environmental causes of illness.

Conclusions

In conclusion, I would like to emphasise again that many of the social and ethical issues raised by advances in molecular genetics are not new, although the scientific knowledge and techniques generated by the new genetics might be. The enthusiasm to exploit the new techniques to their full potential, however, may lead people to forget that the same ethical principles should be applied as in other areas of medicine, one of the most important for an evidence based health service being, as the chief medical officer has recently reminded us "that health interventions do more good than harm and are affordable".[12]

There are, as I have shown, some new issues raised by the new genetics that have received and will receive widespread attention. The same principles should govern the application of advances in genetic understanding as govern the application of advances in other areas of scientific knowledge; procedures should not be introduced simply because they are possible but only because they have been shown to be beneficial.

1 Office of Science and Technology. *Technology foresight programme: report of health and life sciences panel.* London: HMSO, 1995.

2 Department of Health. *Report of the genetics research advisory group: a first report to the NHS central research and development committee on the new genetics.* London: HMSO, 1995.

3 Department of Health. *The genetics of common diseases. A second report to the NHS central research and development committee on the new genetics.* London: HMSO, 1995.

4 House of Commons Science and Technology Committee. *Human genetics: the science and its consequences.* London: HMSO, 1995.

5 Richards JR, Bobrow M. Ethical issues in clinical genetics. A report of a joint working party of the College Committee on Ethical Issues in Medicine and the College Committee on Clinical Genetics. *J R Coll Physicians Lond* 1991; **25**: 284–8.

6 Nuffield Council on Bioethics. *Genetic screening: ethical issues.* London: Nuffield Council of Bioethics, 1993.

7 Beckwith J. The human genome initiative: genetics lightning rod. *Am J Law Med* 1991; **17**: 1–13.

8 Richards MPM. The new genetics—some issues for social scientists. *Sociology of Health and Illness* 1993; **15**: 567–86.

9 Davison C, Macintyre S, Davey Smith G. The potential social impact of predictive genetic testing for susceptibility to common chronic diseases: a review and proposed research agenda. *Sociology of Health and Illness* 1993; **16**: 340–71.

10 King MC, Rowell S, Love S. Inherited breast and ovarian cancer. What are the risks? What are the choices? *JAMA* 1993; **269**: 1975–80.

11 Wilson JMG, Jungner G. *Principles and practice of screening for disease.* Geneva: WHO, 1968.

12 Calman KC. Developing screening in the NHS. *Journal of Medical Screening* 1994; **1**: 101–5.

13 Bekker H, Modell M, Deniss G, *et al.* Uptake of cystic fibrosis carrier testing in primary care: supply push or demand pull? *BMJ* 1993; **306**: 1584–6.

14 Breo DL. Altered fates: counselling families with inherited breast cancer. *JAMA* 1993; **269**: 2017–22.

15 Angastiniotis M. Cyprus: thalassaemia programme. *Lancet* 1990; **336**: 1119–20.

16 Davison C, Frankel S, Davey Smith G. Inheriting heart trouble—the relevance of common sense ideas to preventive measures. *Health Education Journal Theory and Practice* 1989; **4**: 329–40.

17 Bradley DM, Parsons EP, Clarke AJ. Experience with screening newborns for Duchenne muscular dystrophy in Wales. *BMJ* 1993; **306**: 357–60.

18 Vines G. Gene tests: the parents' dilemma. *New Scientist* 1994; **144**: 40–4.

19 Andrews LB, Fullarton JE, Holtzman NA, *et al. Assessing genetic risks.* Washington DC: National Academy Press, 1994.

20 Lippman A. Prenatal genetic testing and screening: constructing needs and reinforcing inequities. *Am J Law Med* 1991; **17**: 15–50.

6 Critical look at clinical guidelines

CYNTHIA D MULROW

Background: what really is a guideline?

Guidelines to help practitioners and patients diagnose and manage medical conditions have been around for centuries. One such example is shown in the box. This guideline was developed to give advice on how to manage patients with less severe forms of apoplectic stroke or thundering apoplexy.[1] It was presented in nine sequenced steps. The main intent of the guideline was to influence practice by providing explicit recommendations about the management of a particular health problem.

The intent of current guidelines is the same. They are "systematically developed statements to assist practitioner and patient decisions about appropriate health care for specific clinical circumstances".[2] A key point, however, in the above standard definition of guidelines is that they are meant to be "systematically developed statements" derived from a comprehensive review and weighing of evidence.

The systematic process of guideline development can vary but usually comprises several steps.[3] [4] These include clearly formulating the scope of the clinical problem, the actual goals of the guideline, and the perspective from which it will be used; identifying and assessing pertinent scientific data in an unbiased manner; integrating and weighing data, taking into account multiple outcomes of importance, soundness or level of evidence, and areas where little or conflicting data exist; drafting summary recommendations that include both beneficial and harmful outcomes and comparisons with alternative diagnostic or

51

Guideline for management of apoplexy

1 Entirely uncover the Patient's Head, covering the reſt of his Body but very lightly; procure him inſtantly very freſh free Air, and leave his Neck quite unbound and open

2 His Head ſhould be placed as high as may be, with his Feet hanging down

3 He muſt loſe from twelve to ſixteen Ounces of Blood, and from a free open Orfice in the Arm

4 A Glyſter ſhould be given of a Decoction of the firſt emollient opening Herbs that can be got, with four Spoonfuls of Oil, one Spoonful of Salt: and this ſhould be repeated every three Hours

5 If it is poſſible, he ſhould be made to ſwallow Water plentifully, and in each Pot of which three Drams of Nitre are to be diſſolved

6 As ſoon as the Height and Violence of the Pulſe abates, when his Breathing becomes leſs oppreſſed and difficult, and his Countenance leſs inflamed, he ſhould take the Decoction Nᵒ. 23; or, if it cannot be got ready in Time, he ſhould take three Quarters of an Ounce of Cream of Tartar, and drink Whey plentifully after it

7 He ſhould avoid all ſtrong Liquor, Wine, diſtilled Spirit, whether inwardly or by outward Application, and ſhould even be prevented from *ſmelling them

8 The Patient ſhould be ſtirred, moved, or even touched, as little as it is poſſible: in a Word every Thing muſt be avoided that can give him the leaſt Agitation

9 Strong Ligatures ſhould be made about the Thighs under the Ham: By this Means the Blood is prevented in its Aſcent from the Legs, and leſs is carried up to the Head

Dr Tissot, 1776

therapeutic approaches, where applicable; and external peer review and revision.

Various methods are used to produce guidelines.[5-7] Differences revolve around the emphasis placed on extensive and formal literature review; reliance on national or local experts; types of skills represented in the guideline panel, and type of group judgment process used to arrive at summary statements. The Canadian task force on the periodic health examination is an example of a guideline group that explicitly links recommendation statements with levels of evidence determined from extensive literature review and critique. Guideline panels sponsored by the

Agency for Health Care Policy and Research comprise experts on methods and content who review and interpret scientific data using evidence based approaches combined with expert opinion. The Harvard Community Health Plan, a large health maintenance organisation in Massachusetts, exemplifies a local guideline effort that relies on internal group judgment and less exhaustive literature review. Guideline members include practitioners who are likely users of the guideline and clinical managers. Formal consensus measures, including a nominal group process followed by a Delphi method, are used to develop the final guideline statement.

Rationale behind the guideline explosion

Although medical guidelines have been around for centuries, the rising popularity in systematically developed guidelines during the past two decades is usually traced to a few factors.[8–10] Firstly, there is a clear recognition that there is simply too much information of varying quality for the individual person to sort through and synthesise. Guidelines represent an attempt to distil a gargantuan body of medical information into a manageable amount. Secondly, significant and unexplained variations in practitioners' practices and in patients' health outcomes raise concern that some are not treated effectively or appropriately. Guidelines are proposed as a means of standardising and improving processes of care so that variations are limited and health outcomes benefited. Thirdly, many countries are having difficulty containing health care costs. There is concern that the contributions of the populace, employers, and government and third party payers toward health care are wasted on ineffective or inappropriate care. Some hope that guidelines will curtail increasing costs, decrease costs, or lead to cost effective care.

Criticisms of guidelines

Despite a strong rationale for guidelines and clear enthusiasm from some quarters, they have been roundly criticised for many reasons.[18–22] These criticisms are extensive, often legitimate, sometimes tiresome, and occasionally even fatuous. Many are tabulated in the box. Regardless of their underlying motive or logic the multiple criticisms merit mention to highlight barriers impeding use of guidelines and reasons that guidelines may not

53

Criticisms of guidelines

"too many, multiple guidelines on same topic, developed with different techniques, reflect special interests, biased, developed in ivory tower, give conflicting recommendations, confusing, based on inadequate data, can't keep pace with new evidence, poorly disseminated, inflexible, simplistic, cookbook medicine, likely to increase regulation, likely to increase malpractice claims, will reduce physician autonomy, likely to increase costs, aimed at groups not individual patients, don't take into account disease comorbity or severity, impractical to implement, don't take into account local resources, ignore practitioners' beliefs and values, ignore patients' beliefs and values, sold as panacea, don't work, over emphasise evidence based knowledge which is only one facet of physician practice . . ."

achieve stated aims. The criticisms can be paraphrased from practitioners' view points.

• "There are over 1500 published guidelines. This is too many and defeats the purpose of helping me keep abreast of information".

• "There are multiple guidelines on the same topic. They are developed by using different techniques that I don't understand. But I do know that different guidelines reflect varying perspectives and underlying motives and special interests".

• "Most guidelines are developed by academics in ivory towers who have no concept of the realities of my everyday practice. They give conflicting recommendations. Rather than guiding me toward less uncertainty and a standard of care, I am just confused".

• "Why should I believe guidelines anyway? They are based on inadequate information. They are out of date by the time they are published".

• "Who ever receives or reads guidelines anyway? Only 50 to 60% of us are aware of national guidelines one year after their release. Those of us who are aware of them often interpret them in different ways".

• "Guidelines are inflexible, simplistic, cookbook medicine. They limit rather than enhance my ability to practise good medicine. They will lead to increased regulation. My autonomy as a physician to order tests and prescribe drugs will be limited. Even worse, if I don't follow guideline recommendations, I may be opening myself up to legal reprisals".

• "If I do all of the things suggested in guidelines, costs will increase not decrease".

• "Guidelines are aimed at the average group of patients. There is no such person. They don't even take into account that patients have multiple comorbidities and varying severity of disease".

• I don't find guidelines useful. They aren't worded clearly. They don't give me the information I need to take care of my patients. They don't present legitimate alternatives. They don't take into account that local resources vary, and I don't have the necessary resources to implement them. Worst of all, they pay no heed to my preferences and beliefs as a physician or to the fact that my patients have their own beliefs and preferences".

• "I became a physician to take care of patients. This requires listening, taking histories, examining, interpreting, counselling, helping change certain behaviours and comforting. There is too much hoopla around this evidence based guideline stuff. Using evidence is only a part and not the most important part of being a physician".

• "They don't work".

Proposed uses of guidelines

Guidelines can have several uses, and what is sought from them may vary depending on whether one is a clinician, consumer, payer, manager, regulator, or politician. One often stated broad aim of multiple developers and users of guidelines is to improve processes of care and health outcomes.[5] [11] [13] [23] The processes of care that many guidelines try to influence are physician practices in recommending and utilising particular preventive, diagnostic, or therapeutic strategies. Less often, guidelines directly target patient or consumer practices. On the other hand, the ultimate health outcomes guidelines always aim to influence are patient or consumer based outcomes such as prevention of disease or reduced morbidity and mortality.

A related but more narrow use of guidelines is simply to inform practitioners and patients and consumers about state of the art thinking in medicine.[24] Some proponents believe that such knowledge will promote consensus and decrease variation in practice as well as physician and consumer uncertainty. Such knowledge may assist practitioners in explaining alternatives and patients in making difficult decisions that require a balancing of potential beneficial and harmful effects. Ultimately, it is hoped that the "knowledge" imbedded in guidelines will lead to improved processes and outcomes of care.

Guidelines can be used to monitor, regulate, or enforce particular practices. For example, agencies and groups interested in quality assurance, utilisation review, or continuous quality improvement can use guidelines as the basis for reviewing processes of care and associated outcomes. Eddy has suggested that knowledge of guideline recommendations be used for assessment before professional certification and for giving credential to practitioners for the performance of certain procedures.[25] Others may use guidelines to regulate care, sometimes by linking guideline compliance to financial incentives, determination of justifiable payment, or punitive actions. Organisations, such as health maintenance organisations in the United States, may consider compliance with guidelines in employment decisions. Although there are examples that show guidelines can regulate care and reduce utilisation and costs, whether such regulatory uses lead to improved patient outcomes is not clear.[8 26]

Finally, guidelines are proposed as mechanisms for reducing costs. They have been used to reduce the risk of conflict between physicians and patients and to decrease litigation and associated costs.[26–28] These uses have been fairly limited and many do not believe that guidelines will be easily converted into legal norms or decreased malpractice costs.[29 30] Rather than decreasing costs per se, enthusiasts propose using guidelines to ensure cost effective care.[31] These proponents suggest guidelines be used to identify treatment that can be withheld; the most cost effective among equally effective treatment alternatives; and alternatives that are more effective yet also more expensive. It is thought that these aims will be achieved if quality and cost are both considered when guidelines are initially constructed. Thus far, few formal evaluations of cost have been incorporated into guideline development or implementation.

Review of evidence that guidelines work

The litmus test of the validity of guidelines is whether they are replicable and feasible in the field, and whether they actually achieve their stated aims. Because the most cited and agreed use of guidelines is to improve processes of care and health outcomes, the evidence that guidelines accomplish this aim will be outlined.

In a seminal systematic review published in 1993, Grimshaw and Russell critically evaluated evidence concerning whether systematically developed guidelines lead to improved process of care and outcomes.[32] This review was recently updated to include 91 evaluations of guidelines.[33] Evaluations used various study designs including randomised trials, block designs, before and after comparisons, and time series techniques. Most commonly tested guidelines focused on care of common conditions such as diabetes and hypertension; preventive care such as vaccinations or strategies for preventing various cancers; and physician prescribing practices or use of laboratory and radiological tests.

Eighty seven of the 91 studies that were reviewed examined effects of guidelines on processes of care; 81 (93%) of these reported significant improvements in practitioner compliance with guidelines. Of the 44 most rigorously designed studies (balanced incomplete block designs, randomised controlled trials randomising doctors, and crossover trials), 43 showed significant improvements in process. Fewer studies (12 of 17) assessing patient outcomes showed significant improvements, though eight of 11 of the most rigorously designed studies do show significant improvements in outcomes such as control of blood pressure and smoking cessation. Magnitudes of effect on outcomes in individual studies were generally modest at best and varied from none to 20% improvement over baseline.

The authors of the above reviews concluded that properly developed guidelines can change clinical practice and may lead to changes in patient outcome. They suggested that whether guidelines work is dependent on the strategies used to develop, disseminate, and implement them. Guidelines that incorporate local or internal skill and opinion were proposed as most likely to be effective. Specific educational interventions with patient specific reminders were proposed as the most effective dissemination and implementation strategies.[32]

Review of evidence on implementation strategies

Recently, three systematic reviews have extended knowledge concerning effective dissemination and implementation strategies.[34-36] The focus of the first review was to identify aspects of programmes in the primary care setting that lead to improved quality of care, costs, or patient outcomes.[34] Thirty six evaluations published from 1980 to 1992 were reviewed; 26 of these were randomised trials. Most studied programmes aimed at providing preventive care; reducing physician ordered services; improving technical processes of physicians; or reorganising and coordinating care through multidisciplinary teams or case managers. A few concentrated on improving continuity of care; reducing costs; or improving patient outcomes. One tried to affect humanism of providers, and none addressed comprehensiveness of care. The main findings of the review were that computer generated reminders, audit and feedback of administrative or medical record data, social influence methods such as academic detailing and opinion leader strategies,[37–39] and shifting workload for specific functions to multidisciplinary teams or members of those teams were effective in improving practice performance. There was no proof that these strategies ultimately led to improved patient outcomes, but only four studies included patient outcome measures.

Davis and colleagues reviewed 99 randomised trials of education strategies designed to change physician performance and health care outcomes.[35] Educational material in these trials usually targeted health promotion and disease prevention or clinical disease management; some of the educational material was based on guidelines. They found 70% of the trials demonstrated variable amounts of improvements in physician performance while 48% of interventions aimed at improving patient health care outcomes produced a positive change. Effective change strategies were reminders, patient mediated interventions, outreach visits, opinion leaders, and multifaceted activities which combined two or more approaches. Audit and feedback with educational materials were less effective, and formal conferences alone were not particularly effective.

Oxman reviewed 102 trials of interventions designed to help health care professionals deliver services more effectively or efficiently.[36] Many of the trials included in his review overlap with those in the above mentioned reviews, with the most commonly studied interventions consisting of audit and feedback or reminders and the most commonly targeted informational areas being management of a health problem, preventive services, prescribing practices, and utilisation of diagnostic tests. Oxman found that most interventions "have been shown to have some effect at least some of the time, but even relatively complex interventions such as outreach visits and use of opinion leaders have at best moderate effects of 20 to 50%".

Although the above systematic reviews do not focus exclusively on implementation of guidelines, they include many studies evaluating dissemination and implementation of guidelines. These reviews give salient lessons. Changing physician knowledge and practice and impacting patient outcomes is not easy. Many dissemination and implementation strategies have only modest effects at best and may work in some settings but not others. Most promising approaches are reminders, patient mediated strategies, and social change strategies that are personalised, involve respected local leaders, and incorporate a high degree of interaction. Combining strategies may be useful, and reorganisation of services and staff may be necessary to affect change.

Conclusions

Guidelines are based on several clear rationales as well as subject to many legitimate criticisms. There is burgeoning evidence to show that they can improve provider practice and benefit patient and consumer outcomes. There is also accumulating evidence to suggest that certain dissemination and implementation strategies can be used successfully to change practice. Available evidence, however, shows that guidelines are clearly not a panacea and they may lead to only modest improvements in care and outcomes.

Reasons why guidelines are not likely to have major effects on care and outcomes are multiple. Firstly, for guidelines to improve outcomes, they must be recommending effective diagnostic, preventive, therapeutic, or rehabilitative practices. If the evidence of effectiveness on which the guidelines are based is non-existent, scant, or conflicting the guideline has little chance of improving outcomes. As guidelines usually deal with clinical problems rather than narrow focused questions, there may be several areas of great uncertainty where evidence based information is missing. Recommendations in this setting may improve standardisation and limit variability in the process of care and even contain costs but have little positive benefit on patients' health outcomes.

Secondly, determinants of the process of care are multiple and complex. Many of these determinants are interactive and interdependent. Examples of important patient, provider, and

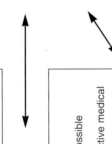

Patients:
- Are at varying stages in their illness
- Have own view of conditions and definitions of health care needs
- Have own beliefs about treatments and outcomes
- Have variable readiness to participate in treatment (compliance)
- Have varying ability to understand and accept different components of health care to weigh risks and benefits
- Have varying acceptance of the authority and knowledge of the treatment team
- Have particular socioeconomic status, educational level, language, sex, age, and ethnicity

Providers:
Awareness
- Are aware of own cultural beliefs and possible stereotypes
- Are aware of cultural influences on effective medical care

Interpersonal skills
- Can communicate effectively with patients
- Are sensitive to patient characteristics
- Respect different types of skill and can function as a multidisciplinary team member

Technical skills
- Know treatment options and possible outcomes
- Are capable of implementing effective treatment processes

Delivery:
- Allows for variation in patient attributes
- Involves participation of and feedback to family and other social support systems
- Coordinates patient and provider goals
- Facilitates prioritisation and sequencing of goals and treatment strategies
- Delivers information, support, and skills necessary to adapt treatments to daily exigencies
- Is feasible for provider and patients
- Is dynamic in revisiting goals and processes and is sustainable
- Is financially and logistically accessible and is environmentally acceptable to providers and patients
- Coordinates components of complex interventions including multiple disciplines and agencies
- Allows for multiple treatment approaches to accomplish goals
- Allows for different information delivery mechanisms (for example, group, audiovisual)

Figure 6.1 Determinants of successful medical care.

delivery determinants of care are given in figure 6.1 (personal communication). Patients have their own beliefs about health care needs, treatments, and outcomes. They have varying ability and desire to understand and accept different components of health care. They have variable readiness to participate in treatment and variable resources and support systems to help carry out recommended treatments. They may have multiple health conditions with competing priorities. They have a particular socioeconomic status, educational level, language, sex, age, and ethnicity all of which may affect the delivery process of care and its outcomes.

Providers also bring their own beliefs, attitudes, knowledge, skills and abilities, and behaviours to the care process. They have varying interpersonal skills and varying abilities in interpreting and dealing with patients' problems. Their access to and ability to use ancillary services may vary. They may understand and value the knowledge and recommendations presented in guidelines in different ways.

The organisational structures and processes that comprise the health care system will affect the delivery of care and outcomes. Obvious important factors are whether care is financially and logistically assessable and is feasible for both patients and providers. Other less often considered delivery characteristics that affect care and outcomes are whether the system coordinates multiple components of complex interventions; allows multiple treatment approaches to accomplish goals; and facilitates prioritisation and sequencing of goals and treatment strategies.

The important message relevant to guidelines is that a more thorough and better understanding of the determinants of the process of care and its outcomes is needed both when composing and implementing guidelines. Emphasis on single provider factors such as impacting knowledge or making evidence based knowledge available needs to be replaced with a more comprehensive approach that incorporates other determinants of provider practice as well as patient and delivery determinants of care and outcomes. As the ultimate aim of many guidelines is to improve patient outcomes, a particularly important issue is integrating patient factors such as their beliefs and needs. Such guidelines should be evidence based but practical and relevant to the needs, abilities, and resources of patients and their providers and health care systems. Finally, while systematically developed evidence based guidelines should be welcomed as critical tools to improve practice and outcomes, they

Overview of guidelines

Uses of guidelines

- Improve care and outcomes

- Improve and assess knowledge

- Regulate and monitor care

- Contain costs and promote cost effective care

Strategies for implementing guidelines

- Administrative changes and rules

- Audit and feedback

- Educational materials and conferences

- Financial incentives or penalties

- Patient mediated interventions

- Reminder systems

- Social influence methods (opinion leaders, outreach visits, local consensus)

- Multifaceted interventions

Processes and outcomes guidelines usually target

- Practitioner—knowledge, skills, behaviour, satisfaction

- Patient—knowledge, behaviour, function, complications, mortality

- System—use, reorganisation of services or staff, costs

are unlikely to affect many of the determinants of care and do not address all aspects of medical practice, some of which is intuitive and subjective. Systematically developed guidelines can be a valuable aid but not a substitute for good practice.

1 Tissot. *Avis du peuple*. 2nd ed. London: Becket and De Hondt, 1766: 159–61. (Translated by Kirkpatrick J.)
2 Field MJ, Lohr KN, eds. *Clinical practice guidelines: directions for a new agency.* Washington DC: Institute of Medicine, National Academy Press, 1990.
3 Woolf SH. Practice guidelines, a new reality in medicine. II. Methods of developing guidelines. *Arch Intern Med* 1992; **152**: 946–52.
4 Evidence Based Care Research Group. Evidence-based care. 2. Setting guidelines: how should we manage this problem? *Can Med Assoc J* 1994; **150**: 1417–23.
5 Audet AM, Greenfield S, Field M. Medical practice guidelines: current activities and future directions. *Ann Inter Med* 1990; **113**: 709–14.
6 Clinton JJ, McCormick K, Besteman J. Enhancing clinical practice. The role of practice guidelines. *Am Psychol* 1994; **49**: 30–3.
7 Olson CM. Consensus statements: applying structure [editorial]. *JAMA* 1995; **273**: 72.
8 Woolf SH. Practice guidelines, a new reality in medicine. I. Recent developments. *Arch Inter Med* 1990; **150**: 1811–8.
9 Humphris D. Clinical guidelines: an industry for growth. *Nursing Times* 1994; **90**: 46–7.
10 Werner M. Can medical decisions be standardized? Should they be? *Clin Chem* 1993; **39**: 1361–8.
11 Tunis SR, Hayward RSA, Wilson MC, *et al.* Internists' attitudes about clinical practice guidelines. *Ann Intern Med* 1994; **120**: 956–63.
12 Gorton TA, Cranford CO, Golden WE, *et al.* Primary care physicians' response to dissemination of practice guidelines. *Arch Fam Med* 1995; **4**: 135–42.
13 Weingarten S, Stone E, Hayward R, *et al.* The adoption of preventive care practice guidelines by primary care physicians: do actions match intentions? *J Gen Intern Med* 1995; **10**: 138–44.
14 Sundall DN. Medical practice guidelines: innovation or failed initiative? *Am Fam Physician* 1991; **43**: 1864–6.
15 Charlton BG. Practice guidelines and practical judgement: the role of mega-trials, meta-analysis and consensus. *Br J Gen Pract* 1994; **44**(384): 290–1.
16 Liang MH. From America: cookbook medicine or food for thought: practice guidelines development in the USA. *Ann Rheum Dis* 1992; **51**: 1257–8.
17 Greer AL. The two cultures of biomedicine: can there be consensus? [editorial]. *JAMA* 1987; **258**: 2739–40.
18 Gilmore A. Clinical practice guidelines: weapons for patients, or shields for MDs? *Can Med Assoc J* 1993; **148**: 429–31.
19 Battista RN, Hodge MJ, Vineis P. Medicine, practice and guidelines: the uneasy juncture of science and art. *J Clin Epidemiol* 1985; **48**: 875–80.
20 Haynes RB. Some problems in applying evidence in clinical practice. *Ann N Y Acad Sci* 1993; **703**: 210–24.
21 Naylor CD. Grey zones of clinical practice: some limits to evidence-based medicine. *Lancet* 1995; **345**: 840–2.
22 Kaegi L. How good are medicine's new recipes? The kitchen debate continues. 1994; **20**: 465–8.
23 Perry S, Marx ES. Practice guidelines: role of economics and physicians. *Health Affairs* 1994; **13**(3): 141–5.
24 Woolf SH. Practice guidelines, a new reality in medicine. III. Impact on patient care. *Arch Intern Med* 1993; **153**: 2646–55.

25 Eddy DM. *A manual for assessing health practices and designing practice policies: the explicit approach.* Philadelphia: American College of Physicians, 1992.

26 Farmer A. Medical practice guidelines: lessons from the United States. *BMJ* 1993; **307**: 313–7.

27 Thomasson GO. Participatory risk management: promoting physician compliance with practice guidelines. *Journal of Quality Improvement* 1994; **20**: 317–29.

28 Garnick DW, Hendricks AM, Brennan TA. Can practice guidelines reduce the number and costs of malpractice claims? *JAMA* 1991; **266**: 2856–60.

29 Merz SM. Clinical practice guidelines: policy issues and legal implications. *Journal of Quality Improvement* 1993; **19**: 306–12.

30 Jutras D. Clinical practice guidelines as legal norms. *Can Med Assoc J* 1993; **148**: 905–8.

31 Shapiro DW, Lasker RD, Bindman AB, *et al.* Containing costs while improving quality of care: the role of profiling and practice guidelines. *Annual Review of Public Health* 1993; **14**: 219–41.

32 Grimshaw JM, Russell LT. Effect of clinical guidelines on medical practice: a systematic review of rigorous evaluations. *Lancet* 1993; **342**: 1317–22.

33 Grimshaw J, Freemantle N, Wallace S, *et al.* Effectiveness bulletin. Developing and implementing clinical practice guidelines. *Quality in Health Care* 1995; **4**: 55–65.

34 Yano EM, Fink A, Hirsch SH, *et al.* Helping practices reach primary care goals. Lessons from the literature. *Arch Intern Med* 1995; **155**: 1146–56.

35 Davis DA, Thomson MA, Oxman AD, *et al.* Changing physician performance: a systematic review of the effect of continuing medical education strategies. *JAMA* 1995; **274**: 700–4.

36 Oxman AD, Thomson MA, Haynes RB, *et al.* No magic bullets: a systematic review of 102 trials of interventions to help health care professionals deliver services more effectively and efficiently. *Can Med Assoc J* (in press).

37 Anderson G. Implementing practice guidelines. *Can Med Assoc J* 1993; **148**: 753–5.

38 Mittman BS, Tonesk X, Jacobson PD. Implementing clinical practice guidelines: social influence strategies and practitioner behaviour change. *Quality Review Bulletin* 1992; **18**(12): 413–21.

39 Soumerai SB, Avorn J. Principles of educational outreach ('academic detailing') to improve clinical decision making. *JAMA* 1990; **263**: 549–56.

7 The Harvard clinical effectiveness training programme

THOMAS H LEE, LEE GOLDMAN,
E FRANCIS COOK, HOWARD HIATT

A landmark paper by James B Wyngaarden was published in 1979 with the ominous title *The Clinical Investigator as an Endangered Species*.[1] Wyngaarden noted a decline in interest in biomedical research by young physicians and warned that unless measures were taken to encourage talented physicians to pursue research, opportunities would be lost. Nearly two decades later the problems described by Wyngaarden and others[2–5] persist, and about 5% of physician investigators in the United States end their research careers every year.[6] Factors that are often cited as reasons for leaving clinical research include inadequate preparation, difficulty in gaining research support, and clinical responsibilities that do not permit sufficient time for the performance of research.[7]

Although several programmes have been developed to support rigorous training of physicians who pursue basic science research, few options are available to physicians who are interested in patient oriented investigation. Increased awareness of the need for more careful examination of the determinants of quality of medical care, however, together with economic pressures on the health care system have intensified the demand for investigators who can study issues such as:
- Risk stratification of patients with common clinical syndromes
- Assessment of cost effectiveness of alternative management strategies
- Measurement of patient outcomes, including quality of life
- Measurement of quality of care.

A critical first step in meeting these needs has been the recognition that patient oriented researchers have needs for training that are analogous to those of physician investigators who perform basic research.[8] These needs include training in research methodologies of clinical investigation such as those listed in the box.

Methodological skills for patient oriented research

- Study design

- Multivariate statistical techniques

- Measurement of comorbid medical conditions

- Assessment of severity of disease

- Measurement of health status and quality of life

- Definition of "appropriateness" of procedures

- Measurement of costs

- Determination of cost effectiveness

- Measurement and improvement of quality of care

Programmes to teach methods in clinical research are now established at some teaching hospitals and are in development at several others.[9] Funding for such programmes is uncertain and highly variable, but important progress has been made in defining optimal models of postdoctoral training for clinical research. These programmes vary in structure considerably, and there is probably no single best strategy for obtaining and integrating these skills for all investigators.

One common feature among the new training programmes at many institutions is their interdisciplinary nature—a reflection of a paradigm shift described by Kelley,[10] in which new "horizontal" relations are formed within a medical centre, crossing the "vertical" divisions defined by clinical specialties and subspecialties. These horizontal relations may be defined by diseases, such as cancer, or by research methodologies. At many universities molecular biologists have developed informal or formal research interactions that may have a more critical role in their lives than their subspecialty affiliations. Analogous cross disciplinary associations are developing among investigators interested in advanced patient oriented research methodologies.

Harvard programme

The Harvard clinical effectiveness programme is among the largest training initiatives for patient oriented researchers. It provides methodological training to postdoctoral trainees during an intensive two month summer session at the Harvard School of Public Health.[11] This programme was founded in 1986 after a Harvard Medical School postdoctoral fellowship training programme for general internists began to attract medical subspecialty fellows from Harvard teaching hospitals. These subspecialty trainees desired instruction in biostatistics, epidemiology, and related disciplines to bring scientific rigour to patient oriented research within their subspecialties.

With support from the WK Kellogg Foundation and the Klingenstein Fund, the clinical effectiveness programme began a formal training curriculum for these subspecialty fellows. The programme has expanded to include 80–90 new enrollees each summer during each of the past few years. Most of the "fellows" are trainees, but nearly one quarter in recent years have been faculty members seeking additional skills. About 15% of the current enrollees are from general internal medicine, another 30–50% are from internal medicine subspecialties, and the remainder are from the other specialties. Most of these fellows come from Harvard teaching hospitals, but nearly half come from other institutions in the United States and hospitals from other countries including the United Kingdom, Switzerland, Germany, Australia, Mexico, Brazil, Canada, Taiwan, and Japan.

A requirement of all applicants is a commitment to an academic career in which the methodological skills of the programme would be applied. All applicants must be sponsored by the director of their clinical subspecialty division, department, or institution, who must guarantee payment for the trainee's tuition for this programme with institutional funds. (Tuition is based on the number of course credits at the Harvard School of Public Health whether or not a trainee enters a formal degree granting track in the programme.) During the programme, enrollees are required to be completely free of clinical responsibilities.

These requirements force the institutions of the candidates for the programme to "screen" the applicants carefully. Domestic applications are not generally interviewed, while international applicants are evaluated via telephone, especially in terms of their proficiency with English. Also, to qualify for a degree from the School of Public Health, an option chosen by more than half of the enrollees, a student must fulfill school requirements for formal testing in English language. These policies have facilitated the enrollment of students who, each year, are characterised by motivation and strong intellectual skills and who are likely candidates for faculty positions on completion of the programme.

Curriculum overview

The "core" of the clinical effectiveness programme curriculum begins on 1 July of each academic year with an intensive seven week summer curriculum that provides 15 credits (out of 40 needed for a Master of Science or Master of Public Health degree) at the Harvard School of Public Health. Required courses are clinical epidemiology (5 credits) and biostatistics (5 credits). Elective courses (2.5 credits) include health services research, decision sciences, outcomes measurements, quality improvement, ethics, and clinical trials. These courses are tailored specifically for the programme's trainees. Thus, the epidemiology course emphasises patient oriented research as opposed to classic population based epidemiology.

Visiting faculty members and fellows who take the summer curriculum usually then return to their institutions, whereas local postdoctoral fellows spend from September of the first year to June of the second academic year (22 months) undertaking their own original research. These fellows often perform their research under the codirection of a senior member of their own clinical division or department and faculty members from the clinical effectiveness programme. During this 22 month period most trainees take additional course work in epidemiology, biostatistics, or health policy and management to supplement their core training. Several of these courses, including an advanced summer course, are designed explicitly for the programme. A seminar course meets weekly throughout the year and provides a forum for students to present "work in progress" or data analyses that have not yet culminated in a published manuscript.

Core curriculum

During the summer core curriculum trainees spend an average of five hours a day (25 a week) in the classroom, and, by self report, require an additional 25–30 hours a week to complete out of class assignments. The courses include workshops and computer laboratories and also emphasise practical skills, such as how to write a grant proposal. Fellows participate in mock study sections during which they review an actual grant proposal previously submitted by one of the programme faculty. During these sessions the "reviewers" are assigned areas of responsibility such as "data quality", "state of the science", and "human subjects". The "reviewers" discuss the proposal in an executive session, pose questions to the proposal's principal investigator, and then assign it a priority score. The goal of these highly popular sessions is to provide the trainees with insight into the mechanics of the grant review process and to encourage them to read a proposal critically.

The clinical epidemiology course includes basic epidemiological principles but also seeks to introduce trainees to all of the steps in performing patient oriented research, including:

- Identification of an appropriate topic
- Review of the literature
- Choosing an appropriate study design
- Definitions of exposure and outcome variables
- Designing a data form or questionnaire
- Pilot test of data collection protocol
- Data collection
- Data management and quality control
- Data analysis
- Abstract preparation and presentation
- Manuscript preparation.

Students are taught in detail the strengths and weaknesses of alternative study designs, including case-control studies, cohort studies, randomised trials, and meta-analysis. Small workshops are used to review published articles.

During the course the trainees develop a research plan for studying a clinical problem of their choice and conclude the course with a presentation of their research plan to the class, including a discussion of the study design, data collection instruments, analytic strategies, and the anticipated problems and limitations. These sessions provide an opportunity for feedback from the faculty and other trainees.

The biostatistics course covers basic quantitive techniques commonly used in clinical research and provides an overview of more advanced techniques. Workshops introduce fellows to the use of microcomputers and appropriate software packages, and analyses are performed with data from actual research projects. By the conclusion of the summer programme fellows should be able to choose and use an appropriate statistical technique for an analysis.

More than half of the trainees take additional courses at the Harvard School of Public Health and ultimately earn the 40 credits required for a master's degree. Up to 10 of these credits can be earned for supervised research. Enrollees, whether local or visiting, can complete a master's degree in epidemiology, for example, by returning for a second summer to take an additional 15 credits and by completing a required research project under the supervision of the programme's faculty.

Conclusions and future directions

Because these trainees are so highly selected the contribution of the clinical effectiveness programme to their future research is difficult to assess. Of the physicians who have enrolled in the summer curriculum and who have finished their clinical training, about 80% are in full time academic positions and another 5% are in government or non-profit research positions.

In the past two years faculty members have noted that growing numbers of enrollees are not seeking futures in the traditional grant supported research track. Instead, these fellows have been sent by their institutions to acquire skills in quality improvement and data analysis, and many return to positions in which much or all of their salary is provided by their hospitals. They are expected to assume major roles in measuring quality of care and patient outcomes and in the development of quality improvement programmes. Because of these needs formal course work in quality management has become an increasingly popular component of the curriculum.

In summary, the needs of patient oriented investigators are analogous to those of bench scientists in that formal instruction in research methodologies can be a critical factor in their development. Also critical are the availability and support of qualified mentors.

On the basis of our experience with the Harvard clinical effectiveness programme, we recommend:

- Recognition that patient oriented investigators require training in specific skills including biostatistics and study design
- Development of cross disciplinary training programmes that can provide formal instruction in these skills to trainees and junior faculty
- Requirement of a minimum commitment by prospective patient oriented researchers of at least two years for research training, including performance of initial investigations
- During research training these fellows should have clinical responsibilities restricted to 20% of their time or less
- Improved support for the career development of patient oriented researchers during research training and early years after training.

1 Wyngaarden JB. The clinical investigator as an endangered species. *N Engl J Med* 1979; **301**: 1254–9.
2 Di Bona GF. Whence cometh tomorrow's clinical investigators? *Clin Res* 1979; **27**: 253–6.
3 Forrest JN Jr. The decline in the training of clinical investigators: data and proposals from the 1970's. *Clin Res* 1980; **28**: 246–7.
4 Thier SO, Challoner DR, Cockerham J, *et al.* Proposals addressing the decline in the training of physician investigators: report of the *ad hoc* committee of the AAMC. *Clin Res* 1980; **28**: 85–90.
5 Gill G. The end of the physician scientist? *The American Scholar* 1984; **53**: 353–68.
6 Institute of Medicine. *Personnel needs and training for biomedical and behavioral research.* Washington DC: National Academy Press, 1985.
7 Applegate WB. Career development in academic medicine. *Am J Med* 1990; **88**: 263–7.
8 Hiatt H, Goldman L. Making medicine more scientific. *Nature* 1994; **371**: 100.
9 Lee TH, Goldman L. Models of postdoctoral clinical research training. *J Invest Med* 1995; **43**: 250–61.
10 Kelley WN. Primary care and subspecialty medicine. Fostering a unified internal medicine. *J Gen Intern Med* 1992; 7: 221–4.
11 Goldman L, Cook EF, Orav J, *et al.* Research training in clinical effectiveness: replacing "in my experience . . ." with rigorous clinical investigation. *Clin Res* 1990; **38**: 686–93.

8 Assessing payback on the investment in research

MARTIN BUXTON, STEVE HANNEY

The importance of assessing payback on the investment in research

Internationally, health care systems are beginning to ensure that services are "evidence based" and "research led". The development in the United Kingdom of the Department of Health's research and development strategy[1] is an example of the movement that believes that there can be a substantial return to investment in health services research. But that belief is not necessarily universally shared; not can it or should it be sustained without its own evidence base.

In support of the research and development strategy the health economics research group at Brunel University was commissioned to develop a model for assessing payback from health services research, and this chapter draws on the ongoing project.[2] It is seen as serving a range of purposes. Firstly, assessment of payback from the examples of completed research could help to strengthen the justification for research expenditure as has been attempted in the United States.[3-4] Secondly, the development of a model might contribute to the prioritisation of future investment in research and development. Thirdly, the modelling might indicate ways of conducting research and research management so as to increase subsequent payback.

The definition of payback and possible measures

Defining and measuring payback has presented intractable problems in many areas of research[5-6] including health research.[7]

To begin to consider measurement it is first necessary to clarify the concept of payback. The concept as used here encompasses at least five main categories of "benefit" from research, for each of which different measures may be appropriate. These categories are summarised in the box and described below.

Categories of payback

a　Knowledge

b　Benefits to future research and research use:
　　i　The better targeting of future research
　　ii　The development of research skills, staff, and overall research capacity
　　iii　A critical capability to utilise appropriately existing research including that from overseas

c　Political and administrative benefits
　　i　Improved information bases on which to take political and executive decisions
　　ii　Other political benefits from undertaking research

d　Health sector benefits
　　i　Cost reduction in the delivery of existing services
　　ii　Qualitative improvements in the process of service delivery
　　iii　Increased effectiveness of services—for example, increased health
　　iv　Equity—for example, improved allocation of resources at an area level, better targeting and accessibility

e　Broader economic benefits
　　i　Wider economic benefits from commercial exploitation of innovations arising from research and development
　　ii　Economic benefits from a healthy workforce and reduction in working days lost

---

Knowledge benefits—Contribution to knowledge constitutes the first step in a rational model of payback. Knowledge may be entirely new, confirmatory, or even simply provide local evidence of a fact long established in world literature. Peer review traditionally has been the key measure of contribution to knowledge; more recently it has been shown that it can be usefully supplemented by bibliometric techniques and patent analysis.[8-12]

Benefits to future research and research use—These can be considerable, although often given less importance. The better targeting of future research could be important[13] and might flow from methodological research and from analysis of observational data.[14] Some indication of this may be provided by citations analysis. The development of researchers with analytical skills, knowledge of the system, and a web of professional contacts is also of major importance; one crude measure of this might be the number of PhDs produced.[15-16] The ability to use or capture existing research, including that from overseas, is a payback from having a sufficiently developed national research capacity.[6]

Political and administrative benefits—These include not just an improved information base but also evidence that decisions (about national or local policies, professional clinical guidelines, etc) were influenced by the improved information base. Surveys of decision makers and analysis of documents might reveal this. Other examples of political benefits include the use of research to deflect criticism by showing the problem is being investigated; to delay immediate decision making; or to justify decisions taken for other reasons.

Health benefits—The benefits might be viewed as the "real" paybacks from the perspective of those running the services and those who need to be convinced of the value of "diverting" resources from provision of services to research and development. These benefits clearly include cost savings, although measurement difficulties arise in estimating whether potential savings are in practice realisable and in ensuring that costs are not simply being transferred elsewhere. Improvements in the process of delivery of care may follow from research, manifested, for example, in reductions in waiting times. Various measures of patient satisfaction exist and contingent valuation techniques are a possible method of assessing the value of quality changes.[17] Greater effectiveness resulting from new or better services may lead to increased health: the "health gain". If the measurement of payback is to be used for comparative purposes this gain will need to be expressed in terms of a common unit, probably a utility construct such as the QALY, which takes account of changes in quantity and quality of patients' lives. Benefits may also take the form of increased equity. Measurement could be attempted by assessing the minimisation of variation in the desired definition of equity. Such definitions have been reviewed as part of the ongoing research on NHS allocation formulas.[18]

Broader economic benefits—These benefits include those resulting from commercial exploitation of innovations arising from research and development. For this aspect of payback methods similar to those used by the private sector to measure returns to research and development may be appropriate.[5 6 19-21] Specific work in relation to technology transfer for health research has been undertaken.[22] Benefits of a health workforce focus on the value of production gained. Typically, a human capital approach has been used in which potential future earnings are calculated for people who, as a result of advances in medical research, can continue to contribute to national production,[3 15 23] but there is a real concern that such measures may overestimate gains in an economy where there is unemployment[24] and that they may have unacceptable equity implications.[25]

A model for assessing payback

Lessons from much of the literature on use of research were drawn on in developing a model. The model uses the restrictive but easily understandable framework of an input-output model, as has been previously used in examining performance measurement in the public sector.[26-28] It provides a means of incorporating the list of paybacks at the points at which they might occur and indicates how research could be oriented to increase these paybacks.

The outline of the model is presented in figure 8.1. The nine steps in the model consist of seven stages (0–VI) and two interfaces (*a* and *b*). The basic concept of an input-output model is extended to incorporate an acknowledgement of the importance of the interfaces between the research system and the wider health system. Points of interface include negotiations between research customers and contractors; brokerage between researchers and the policy community; the involvement of stakeholders; and effective dissemination. These points require a permeability at the

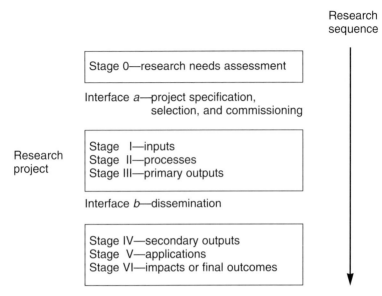

Figure 8.1 Outline input-output model for assessing payback from applied research.

interfaces: there needs to be easy and effective interaction between the project and its environment.[29] The flexible character of the interfaces means it is possible to attempt to apply the model to many types of research ranging from randomised trials to developmental projects. In practice, there are various feedback loops and forward leaps, some of which are described in the text, but for simplicity they are not shown in the figure.

The first stage is deliberately numbered stage 0–research needs assessment, to indicate that these activities occur before the start of a specific project. Currently the United Kingdom research and development programme is devoting much effort to this stage. For example, the work of the standing group on health technology is concerned to identify the priority research needs of the NHS.[30]

The inclusion of interface *a*—project specification, selection, and commissioning, highlights how the model attempts to combine elements of the rational, linear model with a more interactive approach. This takes account of the suggested emphasis on the advantages of researchers helping customers define their needs[29] and the importance of the desirability of negotiations before the research starts about the expected dissemination and use of the research.[7]

At stage I—inputs, it is important to consider not just the financial inputs but also the experience of the researchers, the knowledge base on which they build, and the opportunity costs of their involvement. Even at stage I the interaction between customers and contractors can be important.

Again these points are seen as important at stage II—processes. The model emphasises the desirability of an interactive relationship between customers and researchers during much of the research. Concentration on the appropriateness of the processes to the task in hand also emphasises the importance of the internal norms of science because the rigour of the science is likely to impact on the level of payback. It is also suggested that some outputs and paybacks may flow directly from the processes entailed in the conduct of the research, if, for example, the behaviour of practitioners involved in the research changes as a result of their involvement.

The importance of knowledge (payback category a in box) at stage III—primary outputs—emphasises that this is seen as an appropriate payback and can be measured, in part, by publication counts and citations analysis and will also be subject to more traditional peer review in various forms. Some of the paybacks to future research could also be seen as featuring here. These research benefits, however, occupy a complex place within the model: better targeting is a feedback loop to assessment of needs of future research, and the training of researchers not only helps encourage (within an interaction model) the uptake of research findings but also feeds back as an input into future research. Furthermore, the utilisation or capture of research findings from elsewhere could be seen as an additional input coming at this stage.

The great emphasis given to dissemination in the literature is also drawn on in the depiction of interface b—dissemination. It is important to remember, however, that the research findings form only a part of the knowledge available to decision makers and might well be ignored. There are various possible indicators of dissemination activities, including seminar presentations, workshops and media activities, and decision makers could be surveyed about their awareness of the research.

Stage IV—secondary outputs, is complex because while many of the paybacks occurring here can be seen as political and administrative (categories ci and cii in box), others, including staff development, are not. There can be many types of secondary outputs including: major political decisions on services; smaller but still national decisions in setting health targets; local administrative decisions about purchaser and provider contracts; professional decisions about clinical guidelines.

Measuring paybacks at this stage is difficult. A policy decision apparently in line with research might reflect that the substance of the findings led to the decision; equally it might be that the findings provided policy makers with justificatory ammunition for a decision they would anyway have made for other reasons.

Before most of the final two categories of payback—service and economic benefits—occur, changes in the behaviour of practitioners have to happen. This is seen as stage V—applications. At least two types of assessment are necessary at this stage: firstly, changes in behaviour have to be recorded, and, secondly, an attempt has to be made to see how far any changes are a product of research. Again surveys might be used to measure this and audit data are potentially important.

Finally, at stage VI—impacts or final outcomes—the major assessments of service and economic paybacks (categories *d* and *e* in box) can be made by using various measurements described earlier, including the calculations of cost savings, satisfaction with the services provided, and QALYs. Even where observational measurements are possible, it would still be necessary to demonstrate the link with the research project through attributable changes in use against an assumed counterfactual. What would the world have looked like without the research?

Strengths and weaknesses of the model and payback categories

A case study approach was adopted to test the usefulness of the model and to illustrate the payback categories. In the first phase of the research eight case studies were chosen to reflect a range of types of research and likely payback. They were organised according to the nine steps of the model and a full account of them has been published.[31] The case studies demonstrate that the model can help to identify the various categories of payback and the stages at which payback occurs. Furthermore, several factors associated with high payback were highlighted, most of them reinforcing points found in the literature. These include continuing support from customers; active brokerage; liaison with stakeholders; appropriateness and quality of the research; active dissemination; and working in a research unit.

Certain issues were shown to require further work. The measurement of payback needs to ensure that benefits are not double counted. Even that quantitive estimates of impacts and outcomes must be very tentative. There are unresolved issues concerning how to allocate payback between early research and later research building on the key findings. The implied linearity of the model imposes certain weaknesses—for example, some application (stage V) of the primary outputs (stage III) may be necessary before a professional body will take the decision (a secondary output—stage IV) to issue clinical guidelines.

Using assessment of payback in research prioritisation and research management

If research and development is seen as an instrumental process undertaken not simply out of curiosity but to give a return to the health service, then a process of prioritisation should attempt to maximise the expected payback from the research and development investment. A process of ex ante assessment of the expected payback from competing topics or projects would be required to provide the information for priority setting. Our work to date has focused on priority setting for the assessment of health technology and has proposed a three step process building on work undertaken in North America.[32–35]

This would, for a new technology, attempt to use professional judgment to quantify, firstly, the theoretical potential payback—the potential difference in health gain (and costs) between the new and existing technology. Secondly, to adjust that to reflect expectations of the process of adoption without research evidence. Then in the context of a specific research proposal this in turn would need to be adjusted to reflect how far the results can be expected to change behaviour to achieve the expected potential benefit. This three step process needs further elaboration and testing to see whether it can be turned into a practically useful quantitive tool. Whether or not this quantification is possible, the model can help to clarify what needs to be considered in any existing less quantified process of prioritisation.[30]

Finally the input-output model presented here offers research commissioners and researchers themselves a framework with which to consider the possible categories of payback from a research and development project and the way in which the payback is likely to be achieved. It then can provide a means of considering what action could be taken to increase expected payback and to ensure that the research produces health benefits.

Conclusion

As yet our ability to measure payback and our understanding of the factors that influence it are imperfect. An input-output model "with permeable interfaces" offers a framework within which to consider the problem. The project has identified a possible approach to prioritisation of research and development, but this requires and is receiving further development and testing. What is very clear is that if research and development is to continue to receive increased funding that might otherwise be devoted directly to patient care, this cannot be supported simply in terms of scientific curiosity but needs to be justified by good evidence of the payback on an investment in research and development.

This project is commissioned and funded by the research and development directorate of the Department of Health. We gratefully acknowledge the important contributions of Rachel Elliott, Mary Henkel, Justin Keen, Mark Sculpher, Penny Youll, and the many other colleagues in the HSR community with whom we have discussed these ideas. But, as authors, we remain solely responsible for the views expressed.

1 Department of Health. *Research for health*. London: Department of Health, 1993.

2 Buxton M, Hanney S. *Assessing payback from department of health research and development: preliminary report*. Vol 1. *The main report*. Uxbridge: Health Economics Research Group, Brunel University, 1994.

3 National Institutes of Health. *Cost savings resulting from NIH research support*. 2nd ed. Bethesda: NHI, 1993.

4 Raiten D, Berman S. *Can the impact of basic biomedical research be measured? A case study approach*. Bethesda: Life Sciences Research Office, Federation of American Societies for Experimental Biology, 1993.

5 Office of Technology Assessment. *Research funding as an investment: can we measure the returns*. Washington DC: Government Printing Office, 1986.

6 Office of Science and Technology and Programme for Policy Research in Engineering Science and Technology. *Returns to research and development spending*. London: HMSO, 1989.

7 Richardson A, Jackson C, Sykes W. *Taking research seriously*. London: Department of Health, 1990.

8 Anderson J. *New approaches to evaluation in UK research funding*. London: Science Policy Support Group, 1989. (Concept Paper No 9.)

9 Cabinet Office. *Research and development assessment. A guide for customers and managers of R and D*. London: HMSO, 1989.

10 Cave M, Hanney S, Kogan M, Trevett G. *The use of performance indicators in higher education*. London: Jessica Kingsley, 1988.

11 Commission of the European Communities. *Patents as indicators of the utility of European Community R and D programmes*. Luxembourg: Office for Official Publications of the European Community, 1991.

12 Thrift L. *Research evaluation, social science and public policy: a critical overview.* London: Science Policy Support Group, 1994. (Review Paper No 6.)

13 Gordon M, Meadows A. *The dissemination of findings of DHSS funded research.* Leicester: Primary Communications Research Centre, University of Leicester, 1981.

14 Chalmers I. *Assessing the effects of health technologies. Report from the advisory group on health technology assessment.* London: Department of Health, 1992.

15 Mushkin S. *Biomedical research: costs and benefits.* Cambridge, Massachusetts: Ballinger, 1979.

16 Vehorn C, Landefeld J, Wagner D, *et al.* Measuring the contribution of biomedical research to the production of health. *Research Policy* 1982; **11**: 3–13.

17 Cave M, Burningham D, Buxton M, *et al. The valuation of changes in quality in the public services.* London: HMSO, 1994.

18 Carr-Hill R, Hardman G, Martini S, *et al. A formula for distributing NHS revenues based on small area use of hospital beds.* York: University of York, 1994.

19 Mansfield E. Academic research and industrial innovation. *Research Policy* 1991; **20**: 1–12.

20 Smith K. *Economic returns to R&D: methods, results and challenges.* London: Science Policy Support Group, 1991. (Review paper No 3.)

21 Hutton J, Backhouse R. *Payback from research and development: final report.* London: Battelle Medical Technology and Policy Research Centre, 1994.

22 IMPEL. *Proposals for intellectual property handling and technology transfer in the National Health Services. A report prepared for the NHS executive.* London: IMPEL, 1993.

23 Weisbrod B. *Economics and medical research.* Washington DC: American Enterprise Institute, 1983.

24 Koopmanschap M, Rutten F. Indirect costs in economic studies: confronting the confusion. *PharmacoEconomics* 1993; **4**: 446–54.

25 Drummond M, Stoddart G, Torrance G. *Methods for the economic evaluation of health care programmes.* Oxford: Oxford University Press, 1987.

26 Flynn N. Performance measurement in public sector services. *Policy and Politics* 1986; **14**: 389–404.

27 Klein R, Carter M. Performance measurement: a review of concepts and issues. In: Beeton D, ed. *Performance measurement: getting the concepts right.* London: Public Finance Foundation, 1988.

28 Cave M, Hanney S. Performance indicators for higher education and research. In: Cave M, Kogan M, Smith R, eds. *Output and performance measurement in government.* London: Jessica Kingsley, 1990.

29 Kogan M, Henkel M. *Government and research: the Rothschild experiment in a government department.* London: Heinemann, 1983.

30 Standing Group on Health Technology. *Standing group on health technology: 1994 report.* London: Department of Health, 1994.

31 Buxton M, Elliott R, Hanney S, *et al. Assessing payback from department of health research and development: preliminary report.* Vol 2. *Eight case studies.* Uxbridge: Health Economics Research Group, Brunel University, 1994.

32 Detsky A. Are clinical trials a cost-effective investment? *JAMA* 1989; **262**: 1795–800.

33 Drummond M, Davies L, Ferris F. Assessing the costs and benefits of medical research: the diabetic retinopathy study. *Soc Sci Med* 1992; **34**: 973–81.

34 Eddy D. Selecting technologies for assessment. *Int J Technol Assess Health Care* 1989; **5**: 485–501.

35 Institute of Medicine. *Setting priorities for health technology assessment: a model process.* Washington DC: National Academic Press, 1992.

9 The role of the consumer in health research

Introduction

RUTH EVANS

The National Consumer Council (NCC) is a government funded body set up to champion the interests of consumers of goods and services of all types. Out remit includes use of public services and includes a special brief for people who are vulnerable or disadvantaged. We have a range of publications on health care, reflecting our basic consumer principles of equity, choice, information, representation, redress, safety, and access.[1-4]

Scientific basis of health services

The United Kingdom is moving to an "evidence based" health service—a welcome move, particularly if the "evidence" is based not only on pure science but on the views of those who are served by health care services, technologies, and medicines.

A Department of Health publication *Consumers and research in the NHS: consumer issues within the NHS* discusses issues for research in provision of health services, including patient satisfaction, consumer priorities, differences in perspective between the consumer and the health professional, and how needs and outcomes can be measured, and involving the consumer in research.[5] With respect to the final point, the report notes that "Research is required on the barriers to real cooperation in the research process, and how they can be overcome . . . community involvement has had difficulty in overcoming academic exclusiveness. Even where the consumer is not easily included in the conduct or analysis of research, however, there should be consultation about the research agenda, and honesty about its purposes and potential outcome".

Consumer involvement in research can inform the research agenda in many ways, for instance, about:

- Health services (their organisation and management; provision of different types of health care)
- Uses of new technology, different types of treatment or intervention
- The development of new medicines.

In a 1990 research report the National Consumer Council examined the need for service standards for evaluation of performance to improve service quality.[6] To inform this process we asserted that as a first step consumers' concerns should be established. We worked with two health authorities to test the views of people with dementia and their carers about the services they used and concluded that only through a cycle of action and reaction involving consumers, planners, and providers could we be sure that the planning of future services is geared to consumers' demands. We believe that this principle is transferable to wider issues of research and development in health care.

If consumers do not help to ask the questions about *what* should be researched, and to what ends, the outcome of the research may not take us forward in improving health care.

Consumer involvement can also help consumers be better informed about their own health care—to use the outcome of research to inform choices in health care. Effective involvement in this respect needs appropriate dissemination of information, production of understandable (but not watered down) information accessible when and where it is needed, and breaking down the "protective" barriers which so often mean that professionals or scientists are not prepared to share what they know (or what they do *not* know) with those whose interests they are there to serve.

Progress to date

In the United Kingdom in recent years increasing attention has been paid to the role of the consumer in all aspects of health care. This is welcome, but there is, of course, a long way to go.

Welcome efforts are being made at all levels of the NHS to increase consumer input—from research to management and at local planning levels. In most areas of interest to health researchers, planners, and managers consumers have a vast amount of knowledge to offer. They and their carers are often the ones with intimate and long term knowledge of particular diseases or conditions. Often, however, there are too few resources devoted to enabling consumers to play a meaningful part in health research and planning or inadequate time allowed. For instance, the National Consumer Council and others are often victims of the circulation of voluminous papers at the last minute before an advisory group meeting or consultation deadline.

Consumer input costs time and money. To be effective it warrants consideration of the needs of consumers or those who act as consumer representatives in commenting on or devising the agenda for health research, planning, and provision. The Department of Health identifies areas for research in consumer involvement in *Consumers and research in the NHS: involving consumers in local health care*.[7] Yet putting the theory into practice is not always so easy.

To improve responsiveness and effectiveness of health care we believe that nothing less than infusion of consumer views into the NHS is required. There is need for greater consumer participation and such participation can achieve great success. We believe consumers make an essential contribution to the wider debate about the scientific basis of health care.

The consumer's view

JEAN ROBINSON

Medical care we are offered will increasingly be based on sound evidence from randomised clinical trials. No longer, we hope, will heart attack victims be denied early treatment by life saving clot busting drugs. Women who have had episiotomies will not be stitched with suture material which causes more and longer lasting perineal pain. Not only will the trials be properly conducted, but their evidence will be rapidly disseminated to busy clinicians who will be expected to use remedies which are "efficacious in every case".

But some of us fear that the research and the recommendations will try to fit our sick bodies and minds into a straitjacket of care that is not right for us.

The problems are these. Firstly, researchers try to answer questions which may be important for them, their funders, or the government but which are not necessarily most important for us. Outcome measures are limited and from our point of view, inadequate.

Secondly, most research is short term, and there is too little long term follow up, yet we regard it as essential.

Thirdly, research on what patients think of treatment is not common and is often tacked on as an afterthought rather than being considered and planned as an integral part of clinical studies. When it is done, the quality is variable and can give superficial and dangerously misleading results. Doctors assume they themselves can do social science research (a little home made questionnaire handed out by someone in a white coat or nurse's uniform while you are still in a hospital bed) but would be horrified if a sociologist were to repair a hernia. Clinical research ethics committees often have no members with qualifications in social science and are unable to judge the quality of such studies.

Finally, now that consumer views are considered respectable, indeed essential, in research planning, few consumers have the time or the knowledge to make a really effective contribution. More training is needed. Those of us with some knowledge are already overcommitted in working for the consumers we represent.

Pioneering work by Dr Iain Chalmers and others at the National Perinatal Epidemiology Unit brought researchers and consumer groups together to discuss future research projects, and following that lead consumers have been welcomed into the Cochrane Collaboration.

Childbirth was a specialty in which there were already active and knowledgeable consumer groups like AIMS (Association for Improvements in the Maternity Services) and the National Childbirth Trust. A crucial element in this was that both already had a core of volunteers who were used to reading and criticising medical literature. That is not common in many other specialties to which consumers would like to contribute, though AIDS is a remarkable exception. Sufferers from disease usually raise money for their own charity which is handed over to a medical panel which decides on its distribution.

We soon realised, however, that while we could make valuable and welcomed contributions to improving research projects—for example, helping to ensure that projects were explained properly to patients—the real task, which we are only beginning to tackle, is to get our own research ideas firstly, accepted and, secondly, moved higher up the priority list. This is particularly difficult when research funds are short.

AIMS, in particular, felt that if it were sidelined into merely improving communication with research subjects it could end up providing the "attractive icing on a toxic cake".[8] To give views on a proposed research project and therefore accept some responsibility members would have to read and discuss a substantial amount of the previously published data. Was the literature on thyrotropin releasing hormone really in a state of equipoise, as the *Lancet* leader claimed, so that a trial could ethically go ahead?[9] That could only be agreed if members took time out from other work to look at it and postponed dealing with the increasing number of requests for help from women every week.

There is no doubt that research can no longer be regarded as a specialist field, with grateful patients simply receiving the benefits. For the first time a group of cancer patients who had been involved in a trial criticised its scientific quality[10] and forced the charity commissioners to investigate—and criticise—the work of the funding charities. If consumers are not involved in the planning side they may well end up criticising the published results at the end and telling the grant givers they have wasted their money, and they will be encouraging the public to distrust the results.

However thorough the meta-analysis it may be measuring the wrong things from our point of view. For example, recommendations that routine prophylactic antibiotics for all women having caesarean section reduce infection rates (though not rates for severe infection) and therefore should be standard care, are not wholly accepted by AIMS. While this may be a useful short term measure in some units the studies analysed show huge variations in infection rates, and our priority is that risk of infection should be reduced in the first place. We are also concerned that routine use of antibiotics simply encourages the development of drug resistant bacteria and will result in greater risk for all women. It would be all too easy to read summaries and not the original studies and learn superficial lessons; what is sensible care for the African bush where women come in after long periods of obstructed labour may not necessarily be right for women in the United Kingdom.

A recent government report on "normal" labour in maternity units[11] has recommended that there should be more study of when not if amniotomy should be performed. A multicentre study has shown that it marginally reduces the duration of labour but to no proved benefit[12] As with so may other interventions in childbirth no adequate study of women's views has been done.

One way of improving the quality of the consumer contribution to research is to follow the AIMS policy that anyone who is a research subject should be entitled to see the research results, whether published or unpublished, on provision of a stamped addressed envelope.[13] Not only will this start to redress the power balance and encourage the view that research is done with patients not on patients but it will provide some protection against research fraud.

The role of the consumer in health research in future, as I see it, is, firstly, to embark on a massive self education programme and, secondly, to insist on seats at the planning tables of top medical research units, including the Medical Research Council, royal colleges, and health departments in the United Kingdom, Europe, and the World Health Organisation. The result could be research that is more relevant, more cost effective, and has greater trust from the public on the receiving end of health care.

1 National Consumer Council. Christine Hogg. *In partnership with patients. Involving the community in general practice. A handbook for GPs and practice staff.* London: NCC, 1995 (PD 03/H3B/95).

2 National Consumer Council. *Quality standards in the NHS. The consumer focus.* London: NCC, 1992. (PD 18/H1a/92.)

3 National Consumer Council. *Balancing acts. Conflicts of interest in the regulation of medicine.* London: NCC, 1993. (PD 22/D4f/93.)

4 National Consumer Council. *Secrecy and medicines in Europe.* London: NCC, 1993. (PD 32/D4f/94.)

5 Blaxter M. *Consumers and research in the NHS: consumer issues within the NHS.* Leeds: Department of Health Research and Development Directorate, 1995.

6 National Consumer Council. *Consulting consumers in the NHS. Services for elderly people with dementia living at home.* London: NCC, 1990. (PD 20/H/a/90.)

7 *Consumers and research in the NHS: involving consumers in local health care.* Leeds: Department of Health Research and Development Directorate, 1995.

8 Robinson J. AIMS and the ethics of a clinical trial. *AIMS Journal* 1994; **6**, (4): 1–5.

9 Chiswick M [Comment]. Antenatal thyrotropin releasing hormone. *Lancet* 1995; **345**: 872.

10 Bourke I, Goodare H. Bristol Cancer Help Centre. *Lancet* 1991; **338**: 141.

11 Clnical Standards Advisory Group. Women in normal labour. London: HMSO, 1995.

12 Barrett JFR *et al*. Randomised trial of amniotomy in labour *v* the intention to leave membrane intact until the second stage. *British Journal of Obstetrics and Gynaecology* 1992; **99**: 5–9.

13 Robinson J. A charter for research. *AIMS Journal* 1995; 7, (41).

10 Research in medical ethics and ethics of research in the European Union

ALAIN POMPIDOU

We are now entering the postmodern society. Within the framework of the European Union it is the product of an unavoidable confrontation between experts, politicians, and citizens.

Research in biomedical ethics is justified by the risk of constraint of patients and by the threats to freedom of choice. The development of new biomedical technologies addresses both the very first stages of conception and also the terminal stages of life, not to mention the progress made in biomedical instrumentation as well as in the uses of products and tissues of human origin.

New knowledge thus leads to new abilities and creates new risks. New biomedical technologies lead to new forms of choice for the individual person, the family, and the society in which they live. Characterisation of multifactorial diseases, and in particular of the genes predisposing to diseases, is leading us away from classic preventive medicine towards a so called "predictive" medicine, which threatens the uncertain nature of the pathological risk. The dangers of eugenic practices or the temptations of medicine guided by personal convenience justify research on medical ethics.

This way of thinking ethically is different from personal or professional morality. It is a true morality of actions. Such an ethical code needs to reconcile both one's personal choice and the general interest.

The field of application of this research is wide as it aims to protect the human being from conception to death. This is based on developing responsible attitudes not only by individuals but also by their families or social groups. Such research must assess the risks in light of available knowledge, but it must also try to anticipate potential risks, in particular the so called "indirect" risks whose consequences are not immediately obvious. This kind of research is even more complex in the cases where our knowledge is imprecise or insufficient. It is therefore important to try to assess such risks while relying on two principles: firstly, the principle of caution when seeking to prove the non-harmful nature of a new technology; and, secondly, the principle of learning from experience. It is too often neglected because of the contradictory attitudes of experts: the "enthusiasts" pushing on too quickly and the "critics" putting obstacles in the way ahead. Thanks to an objective analysis, learning from experience allows the achievement of a proper balance between both attitudes.

An ombudsman function among politicians

This shows the need not only for a high standard of training of qualified people in research but also for proper education and training of the public to ensure a true freedom of choice. It will therefore allow a greater acceptance of technical and scientific progress together with its constraints. This implies the need to develop an ombudsman function among the politicians. Today the political decision maker has a major intermediate role between the experts and the lay people. Although the capacity to evaluate risk influences the degree of acceptance of that risk, it is nevertheless important to take account of a certain amount of subjectivity in the assessment of biomedical risk. Personal decision making, however, is acceptable only in so far as it does not threaten the general interest.

Alongside the basic rules of ethics, aiming to respect human rights and to protect the individual, one must equally take account of the sociocultural context and of geoethical aspects, reflecting the perceptions unique to each of the different countries making up the European Union. This is particularly important in as much as it creates a free trade area founded on the free movement of people, possessions, and goods. This requires careful consideration with a view towards better harmonisation of issues concerning the quality and safety of products stemming from new biomedical technologies. A coordinated access to new diagnostic and therapeutic techniques is required as well.

A research code of ethics

Research in biomedical ethics is also based on an ethical approach in the researcher's own thinking that represents a research code of ethics. Although nothing can hold back the progress of knowledge. Scientists, biologists, and medical practitioners must nevertheless provide objective information on the nature of their research, without relying solely on experts or the media. Furthermore, the use of the results of this research must be controlled through legal provisions, if necessary after consultation with the different ethical committees at national as well as at a European level. If medical research is to be at the service of knowledge it is also to be at the service of society to help mankind to progress, both economically and socially.

Conclusion

In conclusion, ethical developments in biomedical research raise the issue of the relations between science, ethics, and society. Biomedical ethics is related to the evolution of society and must involve a multidisciplinary approach. It implies confrontation between scientists, politicians, and public opinion. A strategic orientation of biomedical research policy is now essential. It is based on three concepts: a scientific axis; knowledge, an economic axis; the know how, a sociocultural axis based on past events, across the whole of Europe.

The history of Europe clearly shows our evolution to be based on a reformed humanism. This is an essential element in the ethical progress which aims to identify the place of people in our society and to assess the risk-benefit aspects as well as the financial consequences. A properly adjusted public health policy must intensify the struggle against diseases while respecting our personalities and the high interest of the collectivity to which we belong.

11 Evidence based management in health care

KPD SMITH

The methodologies applied to biomedical and health services research have matured dramatically over the past three decades. Effectiveness, efficiency, and efficacy of clinical practice has been carefully examined in focused areas and is under increasing scrutiny to ensure that the right procedure is delivered to the right person at the right time. The rigour that has developed as a result of the evolution of health services research has not to date been mirrored in terms of health management research. While the number of variables are, arguably, considerably more difficult to control in health management research the introduction via modification of best practice research in clinical service methodologies must be further explored. If such an organised and comprehensive approach to health management is permitted to evolve, the quality of the research and the subsequent application will no doubt dramatically increase. One obvious problem often associated with health management research is that those who are often most self interested in the success of the intervention are, in fact, those leading the evaluation. While this may also be true in clinical medicine, study designs have evolved (for instance, randomised controlled trial with blind intake) that minimise investigator driven bias—a methodological challenge for health management research.

Central to the development of a research driven management system is the acceptance by those involved of contingency theory, which states that there is no one good way to manage and that management is very much environmentally and culturally dependent. Building on this model, the work undertaken at St

Joseph's Hospital and Community Health Centre has confirmed what has been previously identified in the literature: that variables associated with culture, structure, strategy and process, and external environment are essential domains that health management research must consider. While the latter two may well be ascertained by using review mechanisms of strategy and management structure documentation as well as undertaking environmental scan, the first two (culture and structure) pose more difficult problems. Following a review of the literature the approach described by Dr Sandra Dawson, currently at the Judge School of Management, Cambridge University,[1] defines a process in her 1986 book entitled *Analyzing Organizations*, which permits an examination of elements of structures in organisations as well as a schematic model on how one might reveal culture, as well as create culture, in organisations (see box and figures 11.1 and 2). Similarly, Professor Dawson also details a change process model that spans precipitating factors through to outcomes feedback and includes assignation of costs and accruals.

By using this model, organisational data were collected and analysed, the results being incorporated in ongoing strategic planning and visioning processes undertaken by the faculty of health sciences and its affiliated teaching hospitals. Similarly, this

---

Elements of structure in organisations

Specifying individual roles
- Allocation of tasks
- Job definitions

Specifying relationships
- Reporting relationships
- Delegating relationships
- Grouping individuals into teams/departments

Specifying rules and systems
- Control systems and procedures
- Communication systems
- Rules governing terms and conditions of employment
- Rules governing processes of planning and decision making

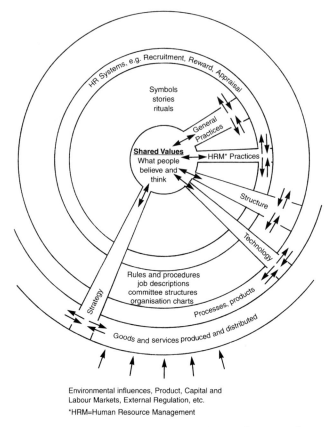

Figure 11.1   Map of the corporate world: how culture may be revealed and created in organisations.

model in totality has been used in the future visioning exercise of St Joseph's Community Health Centre, which is the first hospital sponsored community health centre (ambulatory care centre) in Canada.

In re-examining the research agenda at St Joseph's Hospital, Hamilton, it has become somewhat obvious that one mechanism to ensure enhanced research into health management is to consider each clinical problem and the research associated with it incomplete unless management components and organisational issues are studied as a component part. One must recognise that the primary purpose of such research is for improved quality of care and hopefully enhanced efficiency and effectiveness. It would

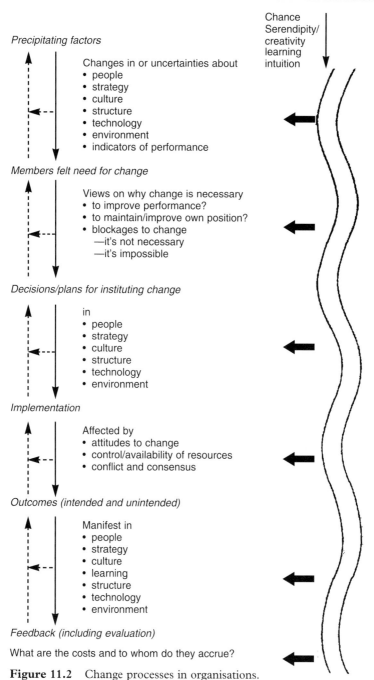

Figure 11.2 Change processes in organisations.

be flawed and dangerous to assume that the purpose of this research might be considered, in a simplistic way, to garner cost saving as its primary purpose. This may be a benefit but must not be the point on which we embark as in so doing, success or failure may be judged inappropriately.

To deliver such a model requires the establishment and mentoring of research teams that are made up of more and different kinds of people than we have seen to date. While the interdisciplinarity of the clinical specialties as well as basic scientists must be continued, the team must be expanded to include managers and academicians of complementary disciplines such as the business sciences (for instance, organisational behaviour), etc. In addition to bringing together unique and diverse pools of talent, this model also enhances the probability of research questions that are investigated with a combination of quantitive and qualitative methodologies—a desired outcome often emphasised in the literature.

The creation and development of such a research team obviously requires significant educational investment on behalf of the individuals and a team as a whole. One mechanism that St Joseph's Hospital, Hamilton, and the faculty of health sciences, McMaster University, have used has been that of management leadership programmes which bring together clinicians, managers, academicians, and experts or mentors in an attempt to provide educational programming and skills development in areas that are complementary to the skill sets of those people involved. The format of these sessions has used principles of adult education with a small group learning format and a problem based approach. Currently under exploration is the opportunity for those particularly interested to undertake two month enrichment experience in areas where they are weakest. For example, managers may well wish to become more familiar with clinical research in an area of interest and equally clinicians may be interested in becoming more aware of management and administrative aspects.

A model for research evaluation and agenda setting

In shifting our focus from one of internal mechanisms to enhanced health management research and evaluation and in building on the research that has been established through clinical medicine with an evidence based medicine model we have borrowed from the work of the Cochrane Collaboration and specifically the work of the Cochrane Collaboration on effective professional practice at the department of health sciences and clinical evaluation, University of York. The model developed by the Cochrane Collaboration aggregated and evaluated the quality of findings, originally by using randomised controlled trial designs but more recently by expanding beyond these. It offers a model for aggregation and evaluation of health management data and also a template by which future research might be evaluated for funding as well as for quality. The standard criteria used to evaluate methodological quality by the collaboration include:

• Baseline characteristics for studies with a second site as a control
• Baseline compliance for studies with a second site for control
• Blind assessment of primary outcomes
• Protection against contamination
• Reliable primary outcomes
• Follow up of professionals (protection against exclusion bias)
• Follow up of subjects.

By a review of the literature, data are extracted independently by two reviewers. Modifying this slightly to permit an evaluation of management literature as well as the following characteristics allows us to borrow from the high quality work undertaken by those participating in the Cochrane Collaboration and introduce the same rigour into health management evaluation that health service evaluation has developed. Those additional characteristics which should be evaluated in an attempt to aggregate findings in health research include:

• Study design
• Inclusion criteria
• Scope
• Consumer involvement
• Characteristics of provider/organisations
• Interventions
• Prospective identifications of barriers to change
• Outcomes
• Result.

By using such a model with the creation of an international research network which has very much begun as a result of the scientific basis for health services conference, a targeted research agenda and international evaluation framework permitting aggregation of research findings could be crafted and supported.

This would also permit the rationalisation of scarce resources and a concentration with those best able to do so in particular areas of management and clinical research. As in clinical medicine, an important outcome will require the application of diffusion innovation theory, which ensures that high quality research findings are appropriately disseminated and incorporated into the practice and operations.

In advocating such a model, I would not wish to imply that little "r" research—that is, research which may in fact simply be confirming the findings of others—should be downplayed or minimised. Indeed, I would suggest that it is the little "r" research that creates a culture conducive and supportive of inquiry as well as stimulates dialogue and questioning across organisations. Thus, it is this little "r" research and those undertaking it who support and permit the application of new findings in traditionally non-academic environments.

Challenges

To achieve some of the objectives described above will require considerable modifications on behalf of a number of organisations. These include medical schools, hospitals and clinical organisations, business and management schools. To achieve these ends requires of us not only the modification of existing training programmes that will introduce clinicians to management and managers to clinical research but also the creation of learning forums throughout undergraduate, postgraduate, and continuing education where these people might come together. The fact that we have been less successful in achieving this in a multidisciplinary sense within and across clinical disciplines should give some concern. A strong steering effect, however, might be realised by granting councils and research funders generally should they encourage this broader research agenda and fiscally support intellectual endeavours which bring together these, to date, unusual teams.

1 Dawson S. *Analyzing organizations*. London: McMillan Press, 1986.

12 A research base for professional staffing of health services

ALISON KITSON, CHRIS McMANUS,
MIKE PRINGLE

Historical roles in health care are changing. This is partly driven by changes in care itself; the clinical role is becoming more complex and demanding, and workloads are ever increasing. Some role changes, however, are due to more fundamental changes in the expectations of whole sectors of the health service. Primary care is shouldering an increasing share of the burden of care at a time when it is being asked to lead commissioning and to undertake research for evidence based medicine.

These changes might be forced in the years to come by changes in medical staffing. Applications for medical posts in primary and secondary care are declining, and many younger doctors are opting either to leave medicine altogether or to take on a lower time commitment than their predecessors. Equally nurses are leaving the profession because they do not think that their skills are being used to best effect, and they are frustrated by not being able to nurse patients properly

This chapter looks at the changing roles of doctors and nurses; it proposes and defines health care teams that will be necessary if we are to adjust to the changing realities of patient care. We will then discuss the implications for primary care, with a final look at the trends in the secondary care medical workforce that will have an impact on the wider picture.

The changing roles of doctors and nurses

The boundaries between the work of doctors and nurses are changing in every health care sector because of a complex range of factors. One reason put forward by many commentators is the move to more cost effective care through substituting expensive professionals with less expensive, competent workers,[1] while others cite quality improvements that occur when tasks are shifted from one group to another.[2] Shifts of boundaries are often precipitated by increasing workload in one group. Recently advances in medical technology and changes in junior doctors' hours[3] and in the training of specialists[4] have noticeably impacted on the provision of acute hospital care. Equally the move in the 1980s of education of nurses from an apprenticeship model to higher education left a large gap in the nursing workforce to be filled by unqualified health care assistants and other support workers.[5]

It must be acknowledged that such profound shifts in roles, responsibilities, and working patterns are based on expediency and pragmatism rather than effectiveness,[6] with few studies examining, for example, doctor-nurse substitution.[7] It has been observed, however, that to the superficial logic that nurses are cheaper than doctors must be added the cost of supervision of nurses by doctors, the volume of activity, and the difference between salary (doctors) and fixed payments plus overtime (nurses).[6]

Early studies have shown that a large proportion of tasks performed by doctors—perhaps up to 70%—could be undertaken by nurses without adverse effects on patient care.[6] These studies are, however, usually single site with small sample sizes and no randomisation; and outcome measures are suspect as are the representativeness of the doctors and nurses involved. Recent studies in the United Kingdom have, however, supported the earlier general conclusions.[2] [7] [8] Nurses taking on medical work improved patient care and improved junior doctors' job satisfaction[2]; nurse led inpatient service for elderly patients was effective[7]; but nurse substitution for junior doctors (the "watered down doctor" model) led to unsatisfactory nurse roles if the nurse-doctor roles were not integrated.[8]

Studies of substitution of care by those not trained in nursing have, on the other hand, found that reducing the number of qualified nurses had an adverse effect on quality of care and patient outcomes.[9–11] It would seem, therefore, that one professional can be substituted for another provided proper training is given—though doubts remain about cost effectiveness when supervision and volume of work are considered—but when professional work is given to untrained staff without proper support, quality of care declines.

The central concern must be how the movement of tasks and responsibilities makes sense in terms of the overall delivery of care to patients. Essentially, if doctors and nurses are to be perceived as highly skilled technicians on a health service conveyor belt then a model based on economically efficient skills training is required; if, on the other hand, multiskilled teams are to be responsible for providing care then several basic principles must be laid down, defining who does what, why, and with what support and training.

Movements of tasks at the boundary can have undesirable consequences. Short[12] and Bradshaw[13] both write about the loss of basic nursing skills such as caring for frail, sick, and vulnerable patients in favour of a high flown, pseudo academic approach to nursing. The tension between old and new roles, evident on both sides of the boundary (S Pembrey, personal communication)[14] can lead to a lack of team work and a vacuum in the delivery of care in the front line team in acute hospital care and in the community.[15]

It must be clear from the onset if a substitution is task or role based. If it is task based then any technically competent person can be trained to substitute—for example, phlebotomists, surgeons' assistants, and treatment room nurses. If, however, more than a set of tasks is being substituted then much greater clarity is required in understanding the impact such shifts will have for those involved—for example, nurse practitioners, nurse specialists, and nurse led units.

The underlying principle should be that most interventions should be devolved down to the level where competency equals cost effectiveness. This will happen only if doctors and nurses are encouraged constantly to improve their own performance, apply more innovative ways of caring for people, and are committed to sharing their knowledge and skill. They will require an understanding of the complementary range of skills and abilities of the members of their health care team.

Care can then be delivered by small teams of highly skilled professionals, all expert in the care of, for example, diabetes, supported by a pool of generic workers. In replacing those roles defined by internal boundaries such as ward sister, such a team would acquire flexibility in responding to patients' needs. Some characteristics of such teams, based on integrated professional roles, can be described.

Integrated professional roles

Doctors and nurses working in health care teams must move away from routine responses in solving clinical problems to formulating those problems in a series of answerable questions, the solutions to which can be implemented in practice. The contribution of all members of the health care team must be considered in determining the effective implementation of solutions into practice. Teams will require the ability to integrate epidemiological and biostatistical skills with clinical experience to ensure that the correct questions are asked, that available evidence can be located in the research literature, and that their actions are evaluated.

Such a move to evidence based health care is intellectually and economically appealing but requires the erosion of the model in which doctors develop guidelines while nurses and therapists carry them out.[16] All professionals will need to undergo training in evidence based health care, and their new skills will need to be integrated into existing initiatives on shared learning between professions.[17] Shared learning offers greater benefits than intellectual or technical understanding—it has been effective in modifying attitudes and perceptions and introduced reflection, evaluation, critical appraisal of practice, and an understanding of team work.[31]

The move to shared learning has been facilitated by an understanding of core competencies—the artistry, intuition, and moral qualities in delivering care; interpersonal and communication skills, networking, managing confidentiality, and openness; forming cooperative relationships and handling conflict—and organisation changes such as the devolution of training budgets to health authorities; more flexible work practices; the commitment to evaluating the effectiveness of continuing professional development; and the move to evidence based medicine throughout the health service.

Such teams will require supervision just at the time that traditional implicit and informal means of supervising inexperienced staff are being dismantled.[18] [19] As the traditional role of the ward sister changes more medical supervision of junior doctors will be required just at the time that their hours are reducing causing more tasks to devolve to nurses. As resources are limited and workloads are increasing the best intentions of clinical supervision of these nurses are being compromised.[19] New systems of mentors, both medical and nursing, to supervise mixed groups delivering particular aspects of care will be required.

The logical consequence of shared learning, shared supervision, and greater teamwork is a review of the career pathways of professional groups, leading to integration. With increasing specialisation experts from a number of professional backgrounds will emerge as natural leaders with, for example, nurses leading in cardiac rehabilitation, incontinence care, or palliative care. Skills will need to be recognised in terms of remuneration and relationships with colleagues.

Some organisations have been able to integrate medical and nursing roles in an exemplary way, with roles and relationships determined after a careful analysis of how best to provide a service centred on patients' needs. Such initiatives as patient centred hospitals, managed care, and care management have attempted to move professionals from traditional to more integrated roles. Such changes do, however, require a supportive organisation, key members of which have an evidence based philosophy.

Such an organisation will develop an evaluative culture,[20] and this will require an augmentation of the few current methods of measuring outcomes.[6] The move from unidisciplinary to clinical audit and the requirement that national guidelines are multiprofessional in construction, however, will ensure that evaluation has a multidisciplinary perspective. As health service contracts specify levels of care and price, the professionals will need to agree the core ingredients, their quality, and the required competencies for each package of care. This will lead to shared accountability.

Lastly, the clinical care team is increasingly working towards patient centred care. Consumerism is a national phenomenon, and evidence based health care will provide more detailed information about treatments and clinical effectiveness and will make choices including rationing more explicit. The partnership between patients and professionals must, however, be protected to ensure that compassion, integrity, and human caring are not squeezed out. Patients in need of treatment will always be in a vulnerable position as will people who need nurses to look after them.

Skill requirement and organisation in primary health care

These conclusions concerning the movement of boundaries and new methods of team working apply in primary care as well as in acute hospital settings. General practitioners are increasingly using practice nurses to substitute for their increasing workload, with preventive care, chronic disease management, and triage becoming nursing tasks. The nature of general practice—owned and largely managed by doctors who are independent contractors—and its central role in the delivery of primary care, however, offer special opportunities and problems. The past decade has seen both the worst and the best of general practice. From the debacle of the new contract[21] through primary care commissioning and fundholding[22] up to the aspiration for a primary care led health service,[23] general practice has ridden a roller coaster which seems at times to defy gravity and reality. The increasing pressure to practise medicine in which decisions are supported by evidence is occurring in primary care as well. Yet primary care used to rely on others—notably hospital doctors—to supply it with evidence. The inadequacy of this approach can be illustrated by the use of anticoagulation in atrial fibrillation.

A review undertaken by Sweeney and colleagues has shown that the trials that demonstrated the benefits of anticoagulation in atrial fibrillation were conducted on small groups of heavily selected patients in secondary care.[24] It has to be questioned whether this evidence applies to the general population. Until they know better practices will continue to act on the available evidence, but there is an urgent need for evidence from and relevant to the primary care setting.

The research base in primary care has been established only recently. It consisted at first of a few research entrepreneurs who happened to be general practitioners, for example Jenner with his work on a vaccine for smallpox and Mackenzie who undertook seminal research in cardiology. Pickles showed the potential for primary care epidemiology by studying infectious diseases in the Yorkshire dales and was the first researcher of note to be recognisable as a general practitioner of today.

It was not until 1956 that the first university department of general practice was established—in Edinburgh—and 1963 before the first professor of general practice—again in Edinburgh. The first chair in England was created in Manchester in 1972, and by now all British medical schools except Oxford and Cambridge have a professor of general practice. The funding for academic general practice has never been very secure and curriculum time has had to be fought for.[25] [26] The General Medical Council's (GMC) document *Tomorrow's Doctors* puts increasing emphasis on community based teaching and the new proposals for service increment for teaching (SIFT) plan to move resources into primary care teaching. Just as general practice confronts the challenge of generating the evidence to underpin its discipline, it is taking on an increasing role in undergraduate education.

Primary care needs a cohort of skilled researchers. Yet its medical and nursing career structures, unlike those for hospital doctors, do not encourage or value research skills. The old regional health authorities have confronted this problem up and down the country, and various solutions have been proposed.

One model, exemplified by the Trent Focus for the Promotion of Research and Development in Primary Care, is to assist primary care workers to access research training and support. Trent Health has invested £0.5m over two years to offer a region-wide service that offers assessment of educational need, finds and funds research skills training, and offers a support service for early research endeavours. The advantages of this service is that it is available to all primary care workers in general practices or community units.

The Northern region and the South West region have adopted a model that identifies, funds, and encourages a network of research practices. A limited number of general practices, usually with a proved track record of research, are funded for protected research time. The time bought can be that of a general practitioner, practice nurse, or "the team". This model has the advantage that the support is focused on the unit in which the research will occur; it will encourage a research culture in those practices. It does, however, offer a limited vision of the location and mode of future research in primary care. Whichever method is chosen the key understanding is that without support and encouragement primary care cannot miraculously develop a research base to meet its needs.

The rapid changes in primary care have raised questions concerning its staffing and organisation. We are aware of the pressures on recruitment that are building up; vocational training schemes have decreasing numbers of applicants and already practice vacancies lie unfilled.

If general practices are to fulfil the increasing clinical expectations of patients and the health service, while still leading commissioning and education, they will need to review their organisation. There is a need for *real* practice managers—not just puppets who will do the doctors' bidding but managers with the skills and mandates to run the business side of the practice. In some practices the manager is now a partner—an appropriate recognition of a key role which frees doctors and nurses from much of the bureaucracy to concentrate on clinical care and the strategy for management.

As practices begin to resemble the health care teams described in this chapter they will become fit to assume a central role in the health service. To do so effectively they must have the skills and resources to develop their research base, and they must develop the clinical and managerial roles within their primary care teams.

Medical career patterns and choices in secondary care

Amid the trend toward role substitution and boundary blurring there still exists a dearth of information about career patterns and choices of individual people who actually become doctors and nurses. The evidence on hospital medical career patterns and choices typifies the lack of data, which is even more acute for general practitioners, nurses, and professions allied to medicine.

On 30 September 1993 NHS hospitals in England and Wales employed 17 560 consultants 4118 senior registrars, 6803 registrars, and 12 851 senior house officers; in addition in public health there were 125 directors of public health, 366 consultants, 388 senior registrars and registrars, and 27 senior house officers; and in general practice there were 27 991 unrestricted principals, 149 restricted principals, 517 assistants, and 1653 trainees.[27] A total of 72 552 people.

In the autumn of 1993; 11 671 people applied through the Universities and Colleges Admissions Service (UCAS) to study medicine, of whom 4739 entered United Kingdom medical schools. To understand the careers of these future doctors we need to have data on career patterns throughout the health service; and we need to define and create new working teams both in acute care and general practice.

It would seem a self evident truth that any organisation training nearly 5000 people a year, and (including Scotland and Northern Ireland) employing nearly 100 000 highly trained specialists, would have a sophisticated mechanism in process for monitoring the careers of these vital personnel, for predicting future needs and possible excesses or shortfalls, and for deciding numbers of new trainees. And certainly no company of comparable size—Marks and Spencer, Sainsbury's, British Airways—would dream of not having a highly organised personnel department, observing the pleasures and the discontents of its staff, tracking their movements, and anticipating potential problems that might impair the viability and effectiveness of its workforce.

Needless to say, the NHS has almost no such mechanisms in place. Excluding the annual statistical compilations quoted above little else is published about the NHS workforce, and probably little else is collected or analysed. Indeed data from general practice are so poor that primary care cannot, unfortunately, be discussed here.

This dearth of data creates a serious problem for assessing the *scientific* basis of medical career patterns and choices. Science requires data, and they are in short supply for medical career patterns. The problem is clearly seen with one of the major changes in the medical workforce in the past three decades—the rapidly increasing proportion of women doctors. Figure 12.1 shows the proportions of women doctors at various career levels since 1963. Proper annual statistical compilations have actually been published only since 1977,[28] and before that the data are based on occasional ad hoc requests from individual researchers.

One might then compare the proportions of women in different grades and claim that women do not enter the higher echelons of hospital medicine as quickly as they might or ought.[29] This simplistic analysis ignores the fact that a typical consultant, aged perhaps 48, would have entered medical school nearly 30 years earlier. The inertial mass of consultants in post therefore means it will take many years for new female medical school entrants to impact on the overall proportion of female consultants. A crude model can be fitted by plotting the proportion of female doctors at each career level as a function of the average year that they probably entered medical school. Figure 12.2 shows a very different picture from figure 12.1. To a first approximation the proportion of women at all stages of hospital careers increases in parallel with the numbers entering medical school—a conclusion with rather different implications.

But even this conclusion is problematic. Figure 12.2 tries to ask what happened in individual careers by assuming that they are all similar and then guessing at many crucial parameters in the model, whereas modelling them properly requires detailed information on their development. And here lurks the principal scientific conclusion of this analysis: *medical careers, which*

107

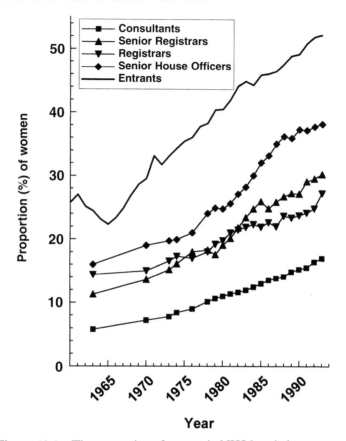

Figure 12.1 The proportion of women in NHS hospital career posts in England and Wales from 1963 to 1993 (C McManus and K Sproston, personal communication). Graphs of this sort have been used to argue that women continue to be underrepresented in hospital careers.

necessarily develop in time, can be modelled properly only from longitudinal data collected through time. And it is those data we do not have. This is surprising as every doctor in the United Kingdom has a General Medical Council registration number, and every hopsital employer has to ask doctors for that number. Tracking the careers of individual doctors ought therefore to be straightforward; it merely seems never to have been done—making planning of the medical workforce nigh on impossible.

The problem lies deeper still. Medical careers start on entrance to medical school, when many decisions are made about careers.

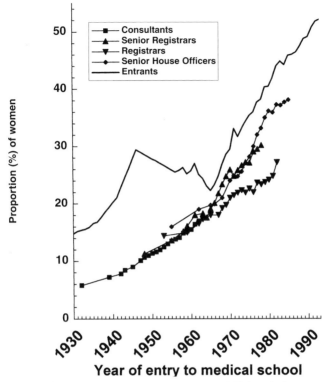

Figure 12.2 The proportion of women in NHS hospital career posts in England and Wales, 1963–1993, plotted in relation to the estimated median year of entry to medical school. The registrar data are somewhat anomalous. In all other groups, however, it is apparent, firstly, that the proportions of women at senior house officer and senior registrar level are broadly equivalent to those at consultant level, and, secondly, that in relation to the proportion of women entering medical school the proportion holding consultant and other career posts in hospital medicine has been rising across the cohorts.

Medical school entrants are not a tabula rasa—they bring with them opinions, attitudes, beliefs, and prejudices, all of which influence career decisions. Returning to the theme of women in medicine, table 12.1 shows not only that few of the final year medical students and preregistration house officers who want to go into careers in surgery are women, but that the same is true of **applicants** to medical school; the implications for increasing the numbers of women surgeons are substantial.

109

Table 12.1 Proportions of female medical school applicants, final year students, and preregistration house officers choosing a particular speciality as their first choice of career. For some specialities there are small numbers overall, and cohorts have been combined where necessary.

Specialty	Applicants*			Final year students		Young doctors†	Preregistration house officers‡
	1981 (n=1014)	1986 (n=1849)	1991 (n=5074)	1981 (n=307)	1986 (n=372)	1966 (n=1453)	1969-75 (n=17 762)
Hospital medicine	52.7% (112)	52.7% (461)	63.5% (1711)	41.8% (79)	51.4% (111)	18.3% (169)	43.2% (3606)
Surgery	24.3% (124)	27.3% (399)	33.6% (1204)	18.9% (37)	25.0% (68)	6.0% (200)	18.9% (2877)
Obstetrics and gynaecology	69.0% (42)	72.5% (160)	75.3% (320)	44.7% (47)		29.5% (105)	59.5% (586)
Anaesthetics	50.0% (26)		34.6% (52)	35.7% (14)		39.6% (106)	55.3% (941)
Pathology	37.5% (88)		53.5% (101)	42.9% (7)		30.9% (55)	59.5% (586)
Radiology/radiotherapy		53.6% (28)		45.5% (11)		30.8% (26)	62.7% (480)
Psychiatry	42.9% (21)	61.3% (106)	61.7% (298)	35.7% (42)		20.3% (64)	55.1% (604)

*Total n at top of column refers to the overall number of subjects responding to the questions on career preferences. Individual numbers in parentheses after percentages refer to number of subjects who named the particular subject (1986, 1991) or who said they had a definite intention of going into the career (1981). The questionnaire also included other careers which are not included here.

†Based on data of Last and Stanley.[30]

‡Based on data of Parkhouse et al.[31]

Longitudinal research on medical career patterns must be long term; follow up from entry to medical school to, say, consultant appointment, necessarily takes 20 plus years, and few funding bodies can think in such terms. Table 12.2 shows the time scales for three current cohort studies by one author (C McM)—a study started in 1980 stretches into the next millennium before all its useful data will be realised.

Training a doctor costs somewhere between the £40 000 estimated in Hansard in 1987[38] and the £200 000 claimed more recently.[39] If a middle estimate of £120 000 is applied to 4500 medical students the total cost is about £600m. Though a modest percentage of this sum would fund the required studies, no one regards this research as their responsibility. The Medical Research Council simply says it is not within its purview; the Economic and Social Research Council is notionally responsible for education research, but its overall budget is pitifully small, and primary and secondary education inevitably have a higher priority; until recently the Department of Health regarded responsibility as lying with the Department of Education, and for it medical education was but a tiny part of its interest. Some charities such as the Leverhulme Trust and Nuffield Foundation have funded some research in medical education, but they can hardly be expected to shoulder the responsibility alone.

Fortunately the Department of Health is now considering a "small research programme" on postgraduate medical education, and the NHS Executive is beginning to ask questions about the effects of undergraduate training. But it is still precious little on which to build a serious science base for understanding medical careers. In the absence of any hard data on careers, we must look at the changing roles of doctors, nurses, and teams and work towards ensuring more appropriate funding for understanding career patterns in each of the professions.

Conclusions

As the boundaries between roles evolve we need to establish new working relationships based on teamwork rather than hierarchies. Such teams will need to have the skills to base decisions on evidence, to share responsibilities, and to evaluate their effectiveness. Nowhere will this be more important than in primary care, where teams of doctors, nurses, and therapists are already struggling to define new working practices.

Table 12.2 Brief details of the three cohort studies of medical student selection and training and the time scale over which such studies must necessarily work.

Detail	1981 Cohort[32-35]	1986 Cohort[35-36]	1991 Cohort[37]
Applicants to	St Mary's	St Mary's	St Mary's, UMDS, UCL, Sheffield, Newcastle
Entrants to	Any United Kingdom school	Any United Kingdom school	Any United Kingdom school
Year of:			
Application	1980	1985	1990
Entrance	1981	1986	1991
Qualification	1986/87	1991/92	1996/97
Five years after qualification	1991/92	1996/97	2001/02
Ten years after qualification	1996/97	2001/02	2006/07
Twenty years after qualification	2006/07	2011/12	2016/17
Thirty years after qualification	2016/17	2021/22	2026/27
No of applicants in study	1478	2399	6901
Proportion (%) United Kingdom applicants	12.6%	24.7%	~71%
No of entrants	517	871	2962
Proportion (%) United Kingdom entrants	12.9%	22.7%	69.7%

UMDS=United Medical and Dental Schools of Guy's and St Thomas's Hospitals.
UCL=University College London.

If, however, the current career patterns of doctors persist the supply of doctors will largely determine the pace of evolution. All clinicians in the health service need to prepare now for new team based working practices. But, most importantly, the health service managers need to be commissioning research that will forewarn them and their clinical colleagues about demographic changes which will dictate the pace of change.

1 Dyson R. *Changing labour utilisation in NHS trusts*. Keele: University of Keele, 1990.
2 Read S, Graves K. *Reduction of junior doctors' hours in Trent region—the nursing contribution. Report to Trent Taskforce*. Sheffield: SCHARR, 1994.
3 NHS Management Executive. *Junior doctors: "the new deal"*. London: NHSME, 1991.
4 Calman K. *Hospital doctors: training for the future*. London: DoH, 1993.
5 UKCC. *Project 2000; a new preparation for practice*. London: UKCC, 1986.
6 Richardson G, Maynard A. *Fewer doctors? More nurses? A review of the knowledge base of doctor-nurse substitution*. York: Centre for Health Economics, University of York, 1995. (Discussion paper 135.)
7 Griffiths P, Evans A. *Evaluating a nursing-led in-patient service*. London: Kings Fund, 1995.
8 Dowling S, Barrett S, West R. With nurse practitioners who needs house officers? *BMJ* 1995; **311**: 309–13.
9 Department of Health and Social Security. *Mix and match: review of nursing skill mix*. London: DHSS, 1986.
10 Robinson J, Stilwell J, Hawley C, Hempstead N. *The role of the support worker in the ward health care team*. Coventry: Nursing Policy Studies Centre, University of Warwick, 1989.
11 Carr-Hill R, Dixon P, Gibbs I, *et al. Skill mix and the effectiveness of nursing care*. York: Centre for Health Economics, University of York, 1992.
12 Short J. Has nursing lost its way? *BMJ* 1995; **311**: 303–4.
13 Bradshaw A. Nursing and medicine: cooperation or conflict? *BMJ* 1995; **311**: 304–5.
14 Dowling S, Barrett S. *Doctors in the making*. Bristol: School for Urban Studies, University of Bristol, 1991.
15 Royal College of General Practitioners. *The nature of general medical practice*. London: RCGP, 1995.
16 Jones J. The machine you see now. *Observer* 1995 April 30.
17 Barr H, Shaw J. *Shared learning. Selected examples from the literature*. London: CAIPE, 1995.
18 Butterworth T, Faugier J. *Clinical supervision and mentorship in nursing*. London: Chapman Hall, 1992.
19 Titchen A, Binnie A. The art of clinical supervision. *Journal of Clinical Nursing* 1995; **4**: 327–34.
20 NHS Executive. *Improving clinical effectiveness*. Leeds: DoH, 1993.
21 Department of Health and the Welsh Office. *General practice in the National Health Service—the 1990 contract*. London: Department of Health, 1989.
22 Secretaries of State for Health, Wales, Northern Ireland, and Scotland. *Working for patients*. London: HMSO, 1989.
23 NHS Executive. *Developing purchasing and GP fundholding*. Leeds: NHSE, Leeds, 1994. (EL(94)79.)
24 Sweeney K, Gray DP, Steele R, *et al.* Use of warfarin in non-rheumatic atrial fibrillation: a commentary from general practice. *Br J Gen Pract* 1995; **45**: 153–8.

25 Howie J, Hannay D, Stevenson J. *The MacKenzie Report.* Edinburgh: Department of General Practice, 1986.
26 Byrne P. University departments of general practice and the undergraduate teaching of general practice in the United Kingdom in 1972. *Journal of the Royal College of General Practitioners* 1973; **23**: suppl 1.
27 Wilson R, Allen P. Medical and dental staffing prospects in the NHS in England and Wales 1993. *Health Trends* 1994; **26**: 70–9.
28 Anonymous. Medical staffing and prospects in the NHS in England and Wales, 1977. *Health Trends* 1978; **10**: 61–4.
29 Lefford F. Women doctors: a quarter century track record. *Lancet* 1987; **i**: 1254–6.
30 Last J, Stanley G. Career preferences of young British doctors. *British Journal of Medical Education* 1968; **2**: 137–55.
31 Parkhouse J. *Doctor's careers.* London: Routledge, 1991.
32 McManus IC, Richards P. An audit of admission to medical school. 1. Acceptances and rejects. *BMJ* 1984; **289**: 1201–4.
33 McManus IC, Richards P. Admission for medicine in the United Kingdom: a structural model. *Med Educ* 1986; **20**: 181–6.
34 McManus IC, Richards P. Prospective survey of performance of medical students during preclinical years. *BMJ* 1986; **293**: 124–7.
35 McManus IC, Richards P, Winder B, *et al.* The changing clinical experience of British medical students. *Lancet* 1993; **341**: 941–4.
36 McManus IC, Richards P, Maitlis S. Prospective study of the disadvantage of people from ethnic minority groups applying to medical schools in the United Kingdom. *BMJ* 1989; **298**: 723–6.
37 McManus IC, Richards P, Winder B, *et al.* Medical school applicants from ethnic minorities: identifying if and when they are disadvantaged. *BMJ* 1995; **310**: 496–500.
38 *House of Commons official report (Hansard)* 1987 November 23; col 81.
39 Allen I. *Doctors and their careers: a new generation.* London: Policy Studies Institute, 1994.

13 Shifting the balance between secondary and primary care

ANGELA COULTER

Governments around the world are engaged in attempts to reorganise health services to cope with increasing demand and spiralling costs resulting from demographic change, technological developments, and rising public expectations. The quest for more cost effective ways of organising health service delivery has focused the spotlight on primary health care. The past 50 years have seen a major expansion in hospital based specialist care, which has consumed an ever increasing share of resources. Primary care has been relatively disadvantaged in this respect. Since it has been recognised that countries with more highly developed systems of primary care tend to have lower health care costs,[1] policies designed to shift the balance of resources back to primary care have been a common theme in health service reforms.

In the United Kingdom, for example, we have seen a number of recent initiatives designed to achieve this shift. After the recommendations of the Tomlinson committee on the future of health care in London,[2] the government embarked on a programme of investment in primary care services in the hope that an expanded primary care sector would be better able to meet health care needs, thus facilitating a planned reduction in the number of hospital beds in the capital. The general practitioner fundholding scheme, in which general practitioners were given budgets to purchase secondary care, was an attempt to shift control of resources to general practitioners in the hope that they would push for greater efficiencies in hospital services and use any savings to invest in their practices.[3] The government has recently

115

announced its intention to extend these initiatives with a general policy to encourage a "primary care led NHS."[4] The details of how this policy initiative will develop are still unclear, but it will probably involve a further extension of the fundholding scheme, together with other measures designed to give general practitioners more control over the way in which priorities are set and resources used.

Financial motives are not the sole reason for attempts to shift the balance of care. Starfield's definition of primary care—"first-contact, continuous, comprehensive, and coordinated care provided to populations undifferentiated by gender, disease or organ system"[1]—encapsulates the main elements that the policy aims to preserve. A health care system in which secondary, tertiary, and emergency care dominates will tend to be fragmented, discontinuous, and uncoordinated. In the absence of high quality first contact generalist services with responsibility for assessing needs, advising on appropriate management, and deciding on appropriate referral, patients have to find their own way through the maze of specialists. In the United States the failure to develop strong primary care services has resulted in duplication and overutilisation of some specialist services and wide disparities in access to care, as well as very high health care expenditure. The tendency for hospitals to consume an increasing share of overall resources, thus weakening primary care, has been observed in many health care systems.

Other pressures are forcing a re-examination of the role of hospitals. Humanitarian rather than financial considerations were uppermost in the development of plans to close long stay mental hospitals and to replace them with community care programmes. If the quality of care for these patients is to be maintained and improved it is most unlikely that this shift will save money. Domiciliary care for elderly patients and those with chronic illnesses or disabilities is widely perceived to be preferable to institutional care; the promotion of supported independent living in the community is a goal of most long term care, but it is achieved at a cost. Technological advances are also having an impact: improved surgical techniques and changes in professional practice have led to shorter hospital stays and an increase in the use of day surgery and outpatient procedures. Follow up care for patients discharged earlier from hospitals falls to community nurses and general practitioners, but these professional complain that resources haven't followed the patients out of the hospitals.

Attempts to shift the balance of care face powerful political obstacles. The economic imperative to centralise acute hospital services, facilitate technological developments, and achieve economies of scale runs up against vociferous public demand for locally accessible health care. Hospital closures are almost invariably unpopular. This policy dilemma reinforces the need for critical examination of the most appropriate setting for different types of health care, but we lack research evidence to inform the public debate.

It is not difficult to assert a general case for shifting the balance of care. Determining which services should be shifted and achieving a shift in practice is much more problematic. Key issues to be resolved include the following:

- When, and for whom, is generalist care more appropriate than specialist care?
- Which hospital based services can be safely and cost effectively transferred to general practice settings?
- What are the "knock on" effects of investment in primary care? Does an expanded primary care service automatically reduce demand for secondary care or does it have the opposite effect?
- How can general practitioners be persuaded to change traditional referral patterns?
- How can the coordination of care across the primary-secondary interface be improved?
- What are the benefits, risks, and costs of shared care schemes?
- Will general practice and community health services be able to cope with an expanded role?
- How will patients and the public react to the changes?

Some of the answers to these questions can be extrapolated from current experience and research evidence, but most will require a coordinated programme of experimental development and evaluation.

The boundaries are already shifting: some procedures are being transferred from hospital to community settings—for example, many diagnostic tests and minor surgical operations can now be performed in general practice, and hospital at home schemes are being established to avoid hospital admissions and facilitate early discharge; attempts are being made to improve coordination of care across the interface and to reduce the number of patients referred inappropriately to specialist services by developing and implementing referral guidelines; shared care schemes are being introduced for management of chronic disease—for example,

117

asthma and diabetes—for maternity care, and for accident and emergency services where general practitioners or nurse practitioners deal with those patients presenting with "primary care problems"; some general practitioners are experimenting with direct booking to surgical waiting lists, avoiding the need for outpatient consultations; and of course general practitioner fundholding schemes, and the more radical development of total purchasing for general practitioners, are now widespread in the United Kingdom, with similar schemes being adopted in Scandinavia, New Zealand, and elsewhere.

Many of these schemes are interesting developments, attracting enthusiastic praise from patients and professionals. But to what extent will they be successful both in improving patient care and achieving a real shift in resources? If this was occurring, one would expect to find evidence of substitution, in other words the new primary care based services could cater effectively for patients who would otherwise have been referred to specialists. Shifting the balance will entail reducing the demand for hospital care.

The following examples illustrate some of the difficulties involved in trying to shift the balance of care.

Preventing unnecessary referrals

There is plenty of evidence that general practitioners' referral rates vary widely and that these variations are hard to explain.[5] Despite a widespread assumption that high referring general practitioners have a tendency to refer unnecessarily, hence wasting expensive hospital resources or specialist time, studies comparing referrals from high and low referring doctors have not confirmed this.[6] Part of the difficulty lies in deciding when a referral is appropriate. Patients, general practitioners, and specialists have different views on this.[7] Possibly low referrers sometimes fail to refer patients who could have benefited from seeing a specialist. Elimination of referrals deemed to be inappropriate would anyway do little to reduce overall rates.[8] There is some evidence that general practitioners who have particular skill in a clinical specialty tend to have high rates of referral to that specialty.[9] This might suggest that specialist referrals should be increased rather than reduced. The question cannot be answered without studies to compare the cost effectiveness of care in the two settings. Unfortunately few such studies have been carried out.

Attempts to modify referral behaviour have usually relied on the development of clinical guidelines designed to assist decision making about when a referral is appropriate. There is sound evidence that guidelines have a useful role in efforts to change clinical behaviour, but they are likely to have an impact on practice only if they are drawn up and agreed by those responsible for implementing them.[10] The problem is that this type of local consensus development is difficult and time consuming.[11] It is an activity for enthusiasts, unlikely to have a major impact on the balance of care unless it is possible to involve most general practitioners and specialists. The absence of evidence on the outcomes of referrals leads to widely differing opinions on when a referral is appropriate, which in turn means that achieving universal consensus on the need to implement referral guidelines is virtually impossible.

Sharing care

Shared or integrated care schemes, whereby general practitioners take over routine care of specific groups of patients with periodic review by consultants, are common in patients with diabetes, asthma, and hypertension and in maternity care. While these types of schemes have obvious attractions, not least to patients, it is not always clear that outcomes for patients are enhanced. A recent review of the evidence on the effectiveness of shared care for diabetes found no advantage for patients over hospital care[12]; costs of well organised diabetic care in general practice are often higher.[13] The Grampian study of integrated care for patients with asthma also found no difference in clinical outcomes between those receiving integrated care and those having conventional outpatient care.[14] Costs to the hospital, the general practitioner, and the patient were slightly lower for the integrated care group and patients preferred the integrated scheme. To extend these schemes will require the adoption of coordinated protocols for the management of diseases and training for the practice staff who will have to implement them. Practice nurses will bear the brunt of the workload, but general practitioners have been slow to invest in training for their directly employed nursing staff.[15]

The open door policy operated by most accident and emergency departments makes them vulnerable to misuse by patients whose needs could more appropriately be met in primary care. There has long been concern, particularly in metropolitan areas, that a substantial proportion of patients attending such departments have conditions that could be adequately and probably better managed by their general practitioner. Many departments operate a nurse triage system to identify the relative urgency of each case, but most patients eventually end up being seen by the casualty officer, who has to assess their needs. This can result in a higher rate of investigation and hospital admission as the casualty officer will be unfamiliar with the patient and his or her social circumstances. Rather than turning patients away some hospitals have experimented with introducing clinics run by general practitioners or nurse practitioners into the accident and emergency department. Where these have been introduced, for example in King's College Hospital in London, they have resulted in lower rates of investigation, prescribing, and referrals to other hospital services, but they have not succeeded in encouraging patients to reduce their use of emergency services.[16] This would require major investment in a public education campaign. Demand for emergency and out of hours care is growing and the services are straining to cope. Most general practitioners are looking for ways to reduce their heavy workload rather than increase it. Reluctance among general practitioners to meet increasing demands for out of hours care may contribute to an increase in demand for hospital emergency services. Somehow the public has to be persuaded of the need to curb inappropriate demand.

Transferring care

In recent years general practitioners have been given financial incentives to perform minor operations in their practices. This usually entails removal of lumps, bumps, and other minor lesions or carrying out vasectomies and other minor procedures. The hope has been that by removing this workload from the hospital waiting times could be reduced for both minor and major operations, but evaluation of this policy has so far revealed no impact on the demand for hospital based minor surgery.[17] The willingness of general practitioners to perform these procedures may have encouraged patients who would not otherwise have done so to come forward for treatment.

The increased availability of near patient diagnostic testing equipment in general practices has had a similarly disappointing impact on demand for hospital services. Rink *et al* studied the introduction of practice based equipment for two biological and four biochemical tests in 12 practices.[18] Investigation rates went up and costs increased; general practitioners seemed to be using the practice equipment as an addition to, rather than a substitute for, hospital laboratory investigations.

Some general practitioners now have direct access to day surgery services. In the Staffordshire scheme, for example, patients requiring day case surgery for conditions such as inguinal hernia, vasectomy, circumcision, hysteroscopy, colposcopy, ingrowing toenail, etc, can be booked directly on to a surgeon's waiting list, avoiding the need for an outpatient assessment. The general practitioner is responsible for the social and anaesthetic assessment of the patient, the patient chooses the date and time of their operation and receives verbal and written information, and the general practitioner arranges the care after the operation. Early reports from this scheme show that patients like it, waiting times are reduced, and at least two outpatient appointments a patient are avoided, as is the need for junior doctor clerking and duplication of recorded information (I Greaves, personal communication). These results are encouraging, but to date these schemes are small scale and restricted to a few well defined procedures. If extended to encompass a wider range of conditions they will have major implications for hospital organisation, deployment of junior doctors, and staffing in general practice. Resources will have to follow the patients back into primary care, but there are few signs that this is occurring at present. The cost effectiveness of such schemes must be established by careful research, not just assumed. A recent review concluded that "the evidence on the efficiency of providing secondary care services in a primary care setting is limited and inconclusive".[19]

General practitioners as purchasers

The general practitioner fundholding scheme is the most comprehensive attempt to date to shift the balance of power, and hence of resources, to primary care. Fundholders have used their financial leverage to achieve a number of beneficial changes—for example, reducing waiting times, securing direct access to certain diagnostic and treatment services, improved turn around of test results, and investing in practice based services such as physiotherapy, counselling, and consultant outreach clinics.[20] There is very little evidence, however, that the hoped for shift in resources has occurred. Despite successfully reducing the number of follow up outpatient appointments, fundholders' new outpatient referrals and hospital admissions are as high as those of their non-fundholding colleagues and still rising.[21] [22] The

121

investment in practice based services has not reduced the demand for secondary care. Indeed improvements in primary care may serve to increase demand because new needs are identified that would previously have gone unmet.

It is clear from these examples that achieving a shift in the balance of care is not going to be easy, and it is not even certain that it will prove to be cost effective. Changes are occurring, but their effect on the overall balance is at best marginal. If fewer routine procedures are to be provided in hospitals in future, capacity to meet health care needs outside hospitals will have to be increased and improved. Specialists will have to do more work in community settings and primary care practitioners (general practitioners and community nurses) will have to expand their role.

The shift will have to be actively managed if it is to proceed smoothly. It will also require careful evaluation. We know too little about the relative cost effectiveness of providing care in different settings and by professionals with different types of training. We also need to develop a better understanding of patients' needs and attitudes. There is some evidence that patients' expectations of the benefits and availability of specialist care are rising.[23] Patients' perceptions of the need for specialist opinion may be an important influence on general practitioners' referral decisions.[9] It may be that primary care is not an acceptable substitute for secondary care in the popular imagination. If a shift is to be secured it will require a culture change among both professionals and the public, and it will be important to ensure that money follows the patients back into primary care.

1 Starfield B. Is primary care essential? *Lancet* 1994; **344**: 1129–33.
2 Tomlinson B. *Report of the inquiry into London's health service, medical education and research.* London: HMSO, 1992.
3 Secretaries of State for Health, Wales, Northern Ireland, and Scotland. *Working for patients.* London: HMSO, 1989.
4 NHS Executive. *Developing NHS purchasing and GP fundholding: towards a primary care-led NHS.* London. HMSO, 1994. (EL(94)79, October 1994.)
5 Wilkin D. Patterns of referral: explaining variation. In: Roland M, Coulter A, eds. *Hospital referrals.* Oxford: Oxford University Press, 1992.
6 Roland M. Measuring appropriateness of hospital referrals. In: Roland M, Coulter A, eds. *Hospital referrals.* Oxford: Oxford University Press, 1992.
7 Grace J, Armstrong D. Referral to hospital: perceptions of patients, general practitioners and consultants about necessity and suitability of referral. *Fam Pract* 1987; **14**: 170–5.
8 Fertig A, Roland M, King H, *et al.* Understanding variation in rates of referral among general practitioners: are inappropriate referrals important and would guidelines help to reduce rates? *BMJ* 1993; **307**: 1467–70.

9 Reynolds D, Chitnis J, Roland M. General practitioner referrals: do good doctors refer more patients to hospital? *BMJ* 1991; **302**: 1250–2.

10 NHS Centre for Reviews and Dissemination and Nuffield Institute for Health. Implementing clinical practice guidelines. *Effective Health Care Bulletin* vol 1, No 8, 1994.

11 Haines A, Armstrong D. Developing referral guidelines. In: Roland M, Coulter A, eds. *Hospital referrals*. Oxford: Oxford University Press, 1992.

12 Greenhalgh P. *Shared care for diabetes: a systematic review*. London: Royal College of General Practitioners, 1994. (Occasional paper 67.)

13 Diabetes Integrated Care Evaluation Team. Integrated care for diabetes: a clinical, social and economic evaluation. *BMJ* 1994; **308**: 1208–12.

14 Grampian Asthma Study of Integrated Care (GRASSIC). Integrated care for asthma: a clinical, social, and economic evaluation. *BMJ* 1994; **308**: 559–64.

15 Atkin K, Lunt N, Parker G, *et al. Nurses count: a national census of practice nurses*. York: Social Policy Research Unit, University of York, 1993.

16 Green J, Dale J, Glucksman E. "Half the aggro". *Health Service Journal* 1991; **101**: 25.

17 Lowy A, Brazier J, Fall M, *et al*. Minor surgery by general practitioners under the 1990 contract: effects on hospital workload. *BMJ* 1993; **307**: 413–7.

18 Rink E, Hilton S, Szczepura A, *et al*. Impact of introducing near patient testing for standard investigations in general practice. *BMJ* 1993; **307**: 775–8.

19 Scott A. *Primary or secondary care? What can economics contribute to evaluation at the interface?* Aberdeen: Health Economics Research Unit, University of Aberdeen, 1995.

20 Coulter A. Evaluating general practice fundholding in the United Kingdom. *European Journal of Public Health* (in press).

21 Coulter A, Bradlow J. Effect of NHS reforms on general practitioners' referral patterns. *BMJ* 1993; **306**: 433–7.

22 Surender R, Bradlow J, Coulter A, *et al*. Perspective study of trends in referral patterns in fundholding and non-fundholding practices in the Oxford region, 1990–4. *BMJ* 1995; **311**: 1205–8.

23 Coulter A. The patient's perspective. In: Roland M, Coulter A, eds. *Hospital referrals*. Oxford: Oxford University Press, 1992.

14 Advances in communication and information technology: implications for health services

JEREMY C WYATT

Background

Communication and information technologies (C and IT) provide tools for processing and distributing information, which is central to health services. Information is the commodity we all use to make decisions[1]; for example, clinical decisions require two kinds of information: patient data and clinical knowledge.[2] Doctors and nurses spend a quarter of their time, and hospitals 15% of their budget, managing information.[3]

Information in health service organisations needs to consist both of patient or resource utilisation data and knowledge of different kinds, and should flow in directions, from centre to periphery and from outlying organisations to the centre. Because many health service organisations and professions have been slow to realise the potential of C and IT to facilitate these flows, we are only just beginning to exploit their potential of allowing all partners in health care, from consumers and clinicians to managers and policy makers, equal access to the information which is vital to delivering appropriate, accessible, timely, and efficient health care.

Health service developments that make communication and information technology more important

Considering first clinicians and clinical information we need not look far for an explanation of the medical profession's recent interest in C and IT. There are dramatic increases in the amount of data collected per patient, partly because of enhanced diagnostic tools and the shift towards chronic diseases.[2] With interdisciplinary teams and shared care of patients between hospital and community becoming common more clinicians need access to the same patient's data (chapter 13); one option, if records remain on paper, is to entrust them to the patient. The introduction of widespread clinical audit, despite dubious evidence of efficacy,[4] had led to more electronic databases being held by clinical directors (or clinicians). The shift to very large simple randomised trials carried out in more representative settings[5] means that more clinicians are becoming involved in research, with the inevitable extra data collection. Turning to medical knowledge, the quantity of knowledge as measured by the number of biomedical journals is doubling every 20 years.[6] Moves towards continuing professional development, lifelong self directed learning, evidence based medicine, and the implementation of research results (see chapter 15) mean that clinicians are demanding access to this knowledge. While distillates such as practice guidelines are finding increasing favour,[7] they often require information systems to ensure optimal application.[8] One major incentive for the computerisation of primary care in the United Kingdom and elsewhere has been the welcome emphasis on preventive care and comprehensive screening and the need for information systems to manage these effectively.

There have also been important trends forcing managers to install information and communication technology. Cost containment and optimising the use of expensive resources requires accurate timely data, as does the separation of the roles of purchaser from provider, the implementation of continuing quality improvement, evidence based management (chapter 11), technology assessment (chapter 2), and the shift towards a "knowledge-based service". Increasingly, health services are becoming more responsive to local consumers (chapter 9) and trying to eliminate geographical and other variations in levels of provision; all this requires more information exchange.

Recognition of the importance of C and IT

As a result of these pressures in the United Kingdom we have seen mushrooming interest in information management and the potential of C and IT. For example, the cabinet office technology foresight programme (chapter 1) and the General Medical Council (GMC)[9] independently identified improved management of clinical information as a key issue for development. The European Union started a large research and development programme on health telematics as part of its fourth framework programme, and improving the flows of clinical and the quality of other information appears as a theme in several of the NHS research and development programmes. Major clinical journals are carrying series on clinical computing and medical informatics, and some are now linked by electronic mail or the World Wide Web. Thus, even in the more conservative professional groups, the importance of improved information management is being appreciated.

Potential risks of C and IT for health services

Even the sober audit commission was optimistic about the future of C and IT in health care[3]; but such technology is not without its costs.

Poor return on investment

The capital costs of installing hospital information and resource management systems in 200 United Kingdom hospitals was £625m over five years,[10] not all of which was wisely spent.[3] To this must be added annual maintenance per site of up to £0.6m,[11] the costs of staff training, telecommunication and online services, system upgrades, building links to legacy databases, and even replacement of stolen equipment—one district general hospital loses around 10% of its personal computers each year. When substantial funds are invested in C and IT it is often unclear how much benefit results; there is widespread complacency about the effectiveness of information systems,[3] reflected by a surprising lack of rigorous evaluation studies.[8] On the other hand, some clinical systems pay for themselves by helping recover charges for procedures that were previously undocumented.[12]

Breaches of confidentiality

When equipment is stolen it is not just the replacement cost that worries IT directors: data are stolen too. When data about patients or health care professionals fall into the wrong hands by accident, when outsiders break in, or when insiders pry into the affairs of those they are not concerned with for reasons of curiosity or financial gain,[13] problems ensue. Patients become less willing to impart their confidences,[13] staff worry that management is looking over their shoulders, and the quality of data deteriorates until "misinformation" rules.[14]

Failure of access to critical data

If data are relied on, when they are lost because of data corruption, poor quality programs, or hardware failures without adequate back up it can have serious consequences—for example, one patient missed a kidney transplant because their record was lost at the time the graft became available. Total system failures are uncommon, but many health service systems are chronically unreliable because they were not developed with the rigorous techniques common in other safety critical domains such as railway signalling or the nuclear industry.[15] Lack of access to legacy data because of installation of new systems or the aging of data held on magnetic media[16] can lead to discontinuities in charted trends over time or loss of data about a patient's exposure to toxins, hampering epidemiological studies.

Technology push overcoming clinical pull

Sometimes inappropriate technology is installed in health care organisations, perhaps because novelty and technology push overcome the clinical pull, leading to systems which perform functions no one needs or which cannot keep up with inevitable changes in clinical or other practices. This leads to fragmentation, with disconnected islands of automation and the same data being entered up to 13 times during each patient's hospital admission in the recent United Kingdom Audit Commission study.[3]

Other problems

Perhaps more insidious is the risk that C and IT will increase the distance between richer and poorer organisations or countries, denying access to information to those without the infrastructure to disseminate it. Even once the infrastructure is there the information itself may be too expensive for some sectors to afford, resulting in increased polarisation.[17]

The abuse of routinely collected data for "outcomes research" is another potential hazard of building large clinical databases.[18] These pose an enormous temptation to the data dredger; the lingering doubts cast by attempts to correlate therapy with clinical outcomes recorded on large United States claims databases[19] and shadow over the future of epidemiology funding in the United States are warnings of what may result.

A final fear is that C and IT will depersonalise clinical encounters by focusing the attention of professionals on objective data and computer screens; current evidence is that patients prefer doctors[20] but not nurses[21] with computers.

Benefits of existing and emerging C and IT for health services

After this long list of cautions it is necessary to remind ourselves of the benefits of existing and potential C and IT for health service users, clinicians, and managers.

Workstation and user interface technology

One major change in computing has been towards clinical workstations which encourage professionals to explore and have a short learning curve.[22] Such workstations allow:

- Interactive contemporaneous data checking, leading to greater accuracy and completeness of data
- Multiple views of the same data—for example, medical, nursing, or managerial views of a patient record[12]
- Rapid, accurate searches of local and remote data or knowledge bases without detailed knowledge of differing search languages[23]
- Flexible presentation of data, including text, tables, or graphs through the ability to transfer information between database, statistics, presentation graphics, and word processor programs
- Standard coding of data and lists of which items are collected (minimum datasets), making comparative audit and research much easier (for example, the APACHE project[24]).

All of these techniques are currently being used to build clinical workstations to support medical, nursing, and other clinical professionals[25] and executive information systems to support managerial staff. Such systems benefit clinical users in various ways—for example, allowing immediate checks for drug interaction or allergy[26] and saving one minute of medical time per repeat prescription written.[27] Workstation techniques can also be used to build touch screen terminals to help patients and other health service users describe their symptoms (for example, GLADYS[28]) and to gain access to information about risk factors, preventive medicine, or support groups.

Emerging user interface technologies include speech recognition, which offers hands free recording (for example, in the operating theatre) but currently is usable only in quiet environments with vocabularies limited to two to three thousand words, and pen based systems (the user points at objects on a sensitive screen and the device translates hand writing), which have potential for mobile users. We are already beginning to see a change in the demarcation between the workstation and the central computer, with mobile personal data assistants or pen based screens that can communicate by radio with their base, and active badges or other kinds of ubiquitous, "embedded" computing,[29] which may replace much of our paper in time.

Database and data storage technologies

Although widely predicted, the demise of large, centralised computers ("servers") still seems premature. Central storage of a master copy of data and knowledge allows a single up to date version to be available to all,[12] instead of requiring tedious updates by floppy disk or compact disk-read only memory (CD-ROM), and is becoming increasingly attractive with improved networking (see below) and "client server" technology. Nowadays the central database may actually be distributed over servers on several sites but appear as one; industry standards for "open systems" make such interconnecting of computers and databases much easier. As already mentioned, while assembling large databases of patient data for studying epidemiology or rare diseases is an attractive idea, great care must be taken to avoid the many biases that lurk in retrospective or routinely collected data.[18 30]

Optical media for storing data, such as the CD-ROM (capacity 550MB), are more robust and compact than magnetic disks or tapes so can be used to distribute large quantities of data, such as the Medline bibliographic databases to libraries or even doctors' offices, or for keeping a permanent record of clinical notes in document imaging systems. Variants of optical media include the write once read many (WORM) disk, which is not erasable so allows a record of all changes to a database to be maintained indefinitely for legal purposes, and the optical card, which can store 20MB of patient data in a highly portable but expensive form. Cards containing a microprocessor ("smart cards") also have the potential to carry patient data, but the high cost of the readers for both systems (£2000 each in the United Kingdom) has so far restricted application to a few pilots. Cards also have the potential to identify health care workers to information systems to ensure appropriate levels of access to data.

Networking, confidentiality, and communications

The rapid fall in the cost of data transfer on local area networks and increase in the number of sites on wide area networks through developments such as "open systems" and store and forward messaging techniques has made data sharing, interconnection of databases, and remote access to specialist skills possible for non-technical staff. This should help moves towards decentralisation, team working, primary-secondary shared care, and improved, more appropriate access to health care for a greater proportion of the population. Because it allows more rapid turnaround of data, health services should also become more responsive, maybe even with shorter waiting lists.

The dilemma for many professionals and organisations is whether to risk loss of confidentiality by using a public access network (such as any network linked to the Internet) or whether to commission an independent, private network—usually a "virtual network"—provided by a telecommunications company. In the United Kingdom there has been vigorous debate about the planned NHS-wide network,[13] with professional concern about confidential patient data being sent between providers and purchasers at the same time as demands for access to certain Internet facilities by doctors; installing an intelligent "fire wall" between two networks will allow most of these concerns to be resolved. As yet, despite the established value of the Internet links to groups such as the Cochrane Collaboration and academics, there seem to be relatively few Internet resources of value to practising clinicians[31] apart from highlights of certain respected medical journals.[32]

Two related issues are the value of anonymisation of patient data (removing obvious identifiers such as name and postcode) and data encryption to improve confidentiality. Anonymisation sounds good in theory but still often allows security services and others with similar resources to identify individuals by linking several databases.[13] Encryption of messages, especially public key encryption, can make data very secure and also allows the message recipient to know that it was sent by the person who holds the private key—authentication—but it adds to the computing power and network bandwidth required.

Turning to communications hardware, wireless networking and cellular telephones allow mobile professionals to keep in touch, though some devices are banned in hospitals because they interfere with infusion pumps or other instruments. Some ambulance services and airlines are exploiting cellular telephone links to transfer patient data—such as electrocardiograms—to an accident and emergency department for interpretation. This can be extended to remote diagnosis or monitoring—for example, of cardiac pacemakers or haemodialysis patients at home.

Advanced multimedia and telemedicine

The idea of combining conventional text and graphics with recorded sound or video has obvious potential, but apart from a few conspicuous exceptions (for example, PLATO, a poisonous plant identification system[33]) has so far found few genuinely valuable uses in health care. Interactive videodisk systems which help patients understand their disease and explore the implications of alternative treatment options do seem to be of value but require many resources to develop. The same is true of multimedia packages for professional education. Enthusiasts are developing virtual reality packages—for example, to simulate endoscopic surgery—but the equipment and development costs are large.

The combination of multimedia and networking, or telemedicine, is developing rapidly in certain specialties[34] such as teledermatology, which allows patients in rural areas to be "seen" by a central dermatologist, and tele-ultrasound, in which expert obstetricians review the tracings of babies in utero and are able to instruct the remote sonographer about obtaining better views of any suspected defects. A successful pilot has been running from the Isle of Wight to Queen Charlotte's hospital in London and has saved many unnecessary referrals. One problem is the cost of the equipment (approximately £20 000 at each end) and the "ISDN" high capacity links required. Teleconferencing is a more generic technology, allowing remote collaborative work with exchange of printed or video material; it is a much cheaper option (about £1500 at each end) and may be of value in certain clinical specialities, especially in rural areas.

131

Robotic surgery has been attempted in some centres for hip arthroplasty because it is more precise than human machining of bone, but safe, cost effective equipment is still under development. Other applications of "artificial intelligence", however, are becoming more widespread in health services as decision support systems.[35]

Decision support systems

Clinical decisions are often hard, requiring the processing of much patient data and medical knowledge, so there has been considerable interest in developing decision support systems that use various statistical and knowledge based or "expert system" techniques. One of the most widely used applications is electroencephalogram interpreters, with a worldwide market of over $50m annually. Increasing use is being made of simple alerts to remind doctors to perform preventive activities or guide test ordering and as way of distributing guidelines; an overview of 28 trials showed these to be an effective way of changing clinical behaviour.[8] Simple drug interaction monitors are increasingly part of the computer based prescribing systems used by half of United Kingdom general practitioners,[26] and prognostic models such as APACHE[24] and the Glasgow coma scale,[36] derived from data, are used worldwide. Turning to managerial applications, making up monthly staff rotas for nurses within multiple constraints has been transformed in some hospitals by use of constraint logic scheduler programs.

It is as yet unclear where the additional benefits would be of more complex decision support systems with techniques such as "critiquing", in which the system gives comments on the clinician's decision.[37]

Examples of effective, low technology applications of C and IT

It is unfortunate if this chapter gives the impression that every clinician and manager needs a high performance workstation connected to a broad band network to function effectively. This is far from the case; C and IT needs to be used selectively, and effective, low cost applications are easily as numerous as ineffective, high cost systems. The following is a sample:

- Desktop publishing: for newsletters (for example, the monthly evidence based "Bandolier" from Anglia and Oxford Regional Health Authority), posters summarising guidelines for clinic rooms, printed risk scoring trees (for example, for melanoma prognosis[38]), disease or problem specific checklists for data collection, which can improve diagnostic accuracy by 10%[22]

- Mail merge printing: patient specific paper "encounter forms" with printed reminders to perform preventive health checks[39]
- Fax machines instead of email or networks for rapid communication of laboratory results, patient referrals and discharge summaries, journal articles, summaries of current state of the art (for example, National Cancer Institute's PDQ cancer profiles[40]), data forms for multicentre trials,[41] or epidemiology[42]
- Cellular telephones instead of laying land lines: in some terrains this may prove a cheaper and more maintainable option[43]
- Conference telephone calls with loud speaking telephones instead of video conferencing: to assist clinical decisions or continuing education
- Slow scan television over standard telephone lines instead of using telemedicine: for remote opinions such as on skull *x* ray
- Store and forward messaging network instead of client server applications running over a broad band network for referrals, laboratory results, etc.
- Modem for batched data transfer over telephone lines instead of store and forward network—for example, daily transfer of laboratory results from hospital to general practices.

Examples of high tech applications for which evidence of effectiveness is still awaited

To contrast with the above list, this is a sample of the many expensive, leading edge C and IT applications which have been tried in health care with no convincing evidence of clinical benefit:

- Picture archiving and communication systems for "filmless radiography": the cost for an average hospital of £10m seems to outweigh the benefits
- Image processing workstations to "enhance" chest radiographs, etc: the resulting images are often harder for trained radiologists to interpret
- Sophisticated alarms on bedside monitors: these are usually turned off by staff irritated by the deluge of false triggers
- Artificial neural nets[44] for anything other than filtering clinical data or selecting abnormal cervical cells
- Complex stand alone "expert" systems[45]: the future of decision support seems to lie with simple modular reminders and alerts embedded within electronic patient record systems[8 46]

133

- Storage of optically scanned clinical notes without text search mechanisms (such as translating the scanned image into the corresponding text through optical character recognition)
- Routine use of purpose built bedside terminals or pen based systems by clinicians[21]
- Use of smart cards to store patient data on a national level (cost seems to outweigh benefits and as yet there is no single standard[47]).

Conclusions

The chief challenges of C and IT are how to ensure that the pressure of novel, untested technology does not overwhelm clinical and other needs and to develop generic, cost effective, incremental solutions to real health care problems. There are a number of guidelines for effective C and IT projects:

- Involve the system users from the outset: establish a clear, user defined, realistic goal, and capable project management with users in a quality assurance role
- Avoid reinventing the wheel: check the literature, similar reference sites, etc, for solutions which may already exist before embarking on a development project
- If it is possible, avoid in house development; ensure the vendor is able to provide adequate support and continuity; assess the viability of vendors and insist that a copy of the source code for the system is held "in escrow" in case of financial collapse
- Ensure all systems respect prevailing industry and national standards
- Respect organisational constraints on systems: adopt an evolutionary not a "big bang" approach; avoid introducing both new technology and a new task simultaneously, etc.[48]

Clinicians might wish to ask themselves the following questions if they are approached about becoming involved in a system development project.

- What is the clinical goal of the project?
- What measures, apart from improving information management, are necessary to achieve the goal?
- How many data must be collected and how must they be processed to achieve the goal?
- Would design and piloting of a paper proforma be a useful first step?

- Which data need to be transferred to a computer, by whom, and when?
- Will the computer's output be available in a form and at a time and place to assist in decision making?
- How will we measure whether the computer is helping us and our patients?
- How can we "future proof" a system, to ensure it is always in line with clinical practice?

We do need more clinical[49] and managerial involvement in the development of health care information systems and many more evaluations of their effectiveness and cost effectiveness. By anticipating the results of these studies it does seem that major benefits of C and IT in health care will be improved quality of care and responsiveness to the public, though financial savings may occasionally be documented as well.[50] These benefits are similar to those accrued from information technology by industry at large.

1 Shortliffe E, Perrault L, Wiederhold G, *et al*, eds. *Medical informatics*. Wokingham: Addison Wesley, 1990: 554.
2 Wyatt JC. Clinical data systems. I. Data and medical records. *Lancet* 1994; **344**: 1543–7.
3 Audit Commission, *Setting the records straight: a study of hospital medical records*. London: Audit Commission, 1995.
4 Mugford M, Banfield P, O'Hanlon M. Effects of feedback of information on clinical practice: a review. *BMJ* 1991; **303**: 398–402.
5 Peto R, Collins R, Gray R. Large-scale randomised evidence: large, simple trials and overviews of trials. *Ann NY Acad Sci* 1993; **703**: 314–40.
6 Wyatt J. Use and sources of medical knowledge. *Lancet* 1991; **338**: 1368–73.
7 Grimshaw JM, Russell IT. Effect of clinical guidelines on medical practice a systematic review of rigorous evaluations. *Lancet* 1993; **342**: 1317–22.
8 Johnston ME, Langton KB, Jaynes RB. A critical appraisal of research on the effects of computer-based decision support systems on clinician performance and patient outcomes. *Ann Intern Med* 1994; **120**: 135–42.
9 Education Committee, GMC, *Recommendations on undergraduate medical education*. London: General Medical Council, 1993: 3.
10 Dean M. London perspective: unhealthy computer systems. *Lancet* 1993; **341**: 1269–70.
11 Harrison GSM. The Winchester experience with the TDS hospital information system. *Br J Urol* 1991; **67**: 532–5.
12 Bleich HL, Beckley RF, Horowitz GL, *et al*. Clinical computing in a teaching hospital. *N Engl J Med* 1985; **312**: 756–64.
13 Anderson R. NHS-wide networking and patient confidentiality. *BMJ* 1995; **311**: 5–6.
14 Burnum JF. The misinformation era: the fall of the medical record. *Ann Intern Med* 1989; **110**: 482–4.
15 Smith MF. Are clinical information systems safe? *BMJ* 1994; **308**: 612.
16 Rothenberg J. Ensuring the longevity of digital documents. *Sci Am* 1995; Jan: 42–7.

17 Zielenski C. New equities of information in an electronic age. *BMJ* 1995; **310**: 1480–1.

18 Byar DP. Why data bases should not replace randomised controlled clinical trials. *Biometrics* 1980; **36**: 337–42.

19 Anderson C. Measuring what works in health care. *Science* 1994; **263**: 1080–1.

20 Bright S. Nearest and dearest. *Br J Health Computing* 1991; Mar: 58–9.

21 Happ BA. The effect of point of care technology on the quality of patient care. In: Safran C, ed. *Proceedings of the 17th annual symposium on computer applications in medical care, Washington DC, 1993.* Washington: AMIA, 1994: 183–7.

22 Wyatt JC. Clinical data systems 2. Components and techniques. *Lancet* 1994; **344**: 1609–14.

23 van Mulligan EM, Timmers T, van Bemmel JH. A new architecture for integration of heterogenous software components. *Methods Inf Med* 1993; **32**: 292–310.

24 Knaus WA, Draper EA, Wagner DP, *et al.* APACHE II: a severity of disease classification system. *Crit Care Med* 1985; **13**: 818–29.

25 Heathfield H, Kirby J. PEN&PAD (elderly care): designing a patient record system for elderly care. In: Safran C, ed. *Proceedings of the 17th annual symposium on computer applications in medical care, Washington DC, 1993.* Washington DC: AMIA, 1994: 129–33.

26 Wyatt JC, Walton R. Computer based prescribing. *BMJ* 1995; **311**: 1181–2.

27 Sullivan F, Mitchell E. Has general practitioner computing made a difference to patient care? A systematic review of published reports. *BMJ* 1995; **311**: 848–52.

28 Spiegelhalter D, Knill-Jones R. Statistical and knowledge-based approaches to clinical decision support systems, with an application in gastroenterology. *Journal of the Royal Statistical Society Series A* 1984; **147**: 35–77.

29 Weiser M. The computer for the 21st century. *Sci Am* 1991; **265**: 94–104.

30 Wyatt JC. Acquisition and use of clinical data for audit and research. *Journal of Evaluation in Clinical Practice* 1995; **1**: 15–27.

31 Coiera E. Medical informatics. *BMJ* 1995; **310**: 1381–7.

32 Delamothe T. BMJ on the internet. *BMJ* 1995; **310**: 1343–4.

33 Pain S. PLATO solves doctors' poison dilemmas. *New Scientist* 1994; August 13: 18.

34 McLaren P, Ball CJ. Telemedicine: lessons remain unheeded. *BMJ* 1995; **310**: 1390–1.

35 Wyatt J. Computer-based knowledge systems. *Lancet* 1991; **338**: 1431–6.

36 Teasdale G, Jennett B. Assessment of coma and impaired consciousness: a practical scale. *Lancet* 1974; **ii**: 81–4.

37 Wyatt J, Altman D, Heathfield H, Pantin C. Development of Design-a-Trial, a knowledge-based critiquing system for authors of clinical trial protocols. *Comput Methods Programs Biomed* 1994; **43**: 283–91.

38 Aitchison TC, Sirel JM, Watt DC, *et al.* Prognostic trees to aid prognosis in patients with cutaneous malignant melanoma. *BMJ* 1995; **311**: 1536–9.

39 McDonald CJ. Use of a computer to detect and respond to clinical events: its effect on clinician behaviour. *Ann Intern Med* 1976; **84**: 162–7.

40 Van Camp AJ. The many faces of PDQ, the cancer therapy database. *Database* 1992; **15**: 95–8.

41 Akazawa K, Kamakura T, Sakamoto M, *et al.* Patient registration and treatment allocation in multi-centre clinical trials using a fax-OCR system. *Methods Inf Med* 1994; **33**: 530–4.

42 Laporte RE, Akazawa S, Hellmonds P, *et al.* Global public health and the information superhighway. *BMJ* 1994; **308**: 1651–2.

43 Stix G, Wallich P. A digital fix for the third world? In: Moeling J, Press M, Rogers JT, eds. Special issue: *the computer in the 21st century.* New York: Scientific American Inc, 1995: 43.

44 Wyatt JC. Nervous about artificial neural networks? *Lancet* 1995; **346**: 1175–7.
45 Wyatt J. Lessons learned from the field trial of ACORN, an expert system to advise on chest pain. In: Barber B, Cao D, Qin D, *et al*, eds. *Proceedings of Sixth World Conference on Medical Informatics, Singapore*. Amsterdam: North Holland, 1989: 111–5.
46 Heathfield HA, Wyatt J. Philosophies for the design and development of clinical decision-support systems. *Methods Inf Med* 1993; **32**: 1–8.
47 Dick RS, Steen EB, eds. *The computer based patient record: an essential technology for health care*. Washington DC: National Academy Press, 1991.
48 Wyatt JC. Clinical data systems. 3. Developing and evaluating clinical data systems. *Lancet* 1994; **344**: 1682–8.
49 Wyatt JC. Hospital information management: the need for clinical leadership. *BMJ* 1995; **311**: 175–8.
50 Tierney WM, Miller ME, Overhage JM, *et al*. Physician order writing on microcomputer workstations. *JAMA* 1993; **269**: 379–83.

15 Promoting the use of research findings

DANIEL DEYKIN, ANDY HAINES

The purpose of this chapter is to place the implementation of research findings in a policy context, to outline factors that may influence the process of implementation, and to describe a programme to evaluate methods of promoting the uptake of research findings launched by the NHS research and development programme. We relate implementation to the responsibility of an integrated health delivery system, such as the NHS in the United Kingdom or the Department of Veterans Affairs in the United States, for the overall management of its funded research and for ensuring that the health care provided takes into account evidence from well conducted studies.

Who is responsible for implementing the results of scientific inquiry? A deep division underlies the question of whether or not government has an obligation that extends beyond the funding of medical and health services research to include a concern for content, data monitoring, synthesis and evaluation, dissemination, and, ultimately, implementation of research findings. Investigators generally accept that public funding of research assumes that it serves a utilitarian public service: the improvement of our ability to understand the world in which we live and thereby to control more effectively the factors that otherwise limit our comfort, safety, and health. There is debate about whether that goal is better served by self directed (so called "curiosity driven") research or by commissioned research ("needs led"). Investigators who flatly refuse to see directed research as anything other than heavy handed intrusion into the realm of free inquiry run the risk of having their results deemed irrelevant to health policy. Conversely, administrators who doubt the benefit of curiosity inspired research may ignore innovative ideas that arise from the research community. There seems little doubt that policy makers have a legitimate obligation to foster both directed and investigator initiated research which can fulfil complementary roles. That there is a continuing tension between these modes of inquiry is amply demonstrated in the recent report by the House of Lords select committee on science and technology on medical research and the NHS reforms.[1]

We envision a cyclical process in which government initiates and in turn is influenced by sponsored research (figure 15.1). The cycle begins with a clearly formulated statement of the government's purpose in funding research, as the Department of

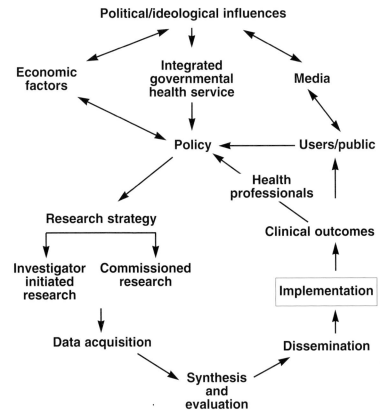

Figure 15.1 Linkages between health policy, research, and implementation.

Health has done.[2] Such a statement might include, but not be limited to:

- Improving the health of the population
- Improving the efficiency and effectiveness of health services
- Improving the quality of governmental policy
- Restraining health care costs.

The next step is a clear statement of research strategy which might include, firstly, the broad objectives of both curiosity inspired and commissioned research (the former aims to allow the creativity, originality, and scientific rigour of investigators full expression; the latter, although also scientifically rigorous, is directed towards priorities defined by the health system); and, secondly, definition of administrative mechanisms to accomplish the research objectives.

Data acquisition must be scrupulously free from external interference. None the less, in the instance of commissioned research, there needs to be monitoring of the process as the construction of commissioning briefs and the peer review procedures can blur an apparently sharp research focus. Data synthesis and evaluation, the critical step immediately before dissemination presents a particular challenge to policy makers. As we have learned from the rigorous methodology required to perform accurate and unbiased overviews of research findings, rules for including and excluding research findings as they apply to policy need to be specified before their publication.[3] The credibility of government's sponsoring of research can be seriously eroded by public perception that findings that might not be welcomed by the sponsoring institution could be systematically suppressed or altered.[4]

Dissemination of research findings and their implementation are closely linked. Traditionally, the scientific community has relied on the time honoured route of presentation in critically edited, peer reviewed journals as the most effective and academically rewarding method for disseminating its findings. As discussed in more detail below, however, the enormous volume of such literature has blunted its effectiveness, and clinicians and policy makers alike are inundated by "information overload". Both governmental agencies and professional societies have responded by promulgating practice guidelines, but as the experience of the Agency for Health Care Policy and Research, funded by congress to construct and disseminate guidelines, has shown the evidence on which to base guidelines is often fragmentary, and, as we discuss below, even the most robust of them may not be accepted if they

140

neglect local circumstances and are introduced haphazardly. The research and development division of the Department of Health has effected an information strategy that relies heavily on the United Kingdom Cochrane Centre and on the NHS centre for reviews and dissemination at York. Both are in early days, and, although high expectations of their output are apparent, it is too soon to evaluate their ultimate contribution. In Britain, as has already occurred in the United States, there is a growing concern over government sponsored promulgation of evidence based practice guidelines. Thus the House of Lords report states, "...the *informed and innovative practitioner must remain free to override 'evidence' if it is either incomplete in the context of the case, or out of date.* We would add that 'evidence' will only express consolidated knowledge; *clinical researchers are constantly enlarging the frontiers of knowledge and must not be held back rigidly within the boundaries of what is known at a particular time*"[1] (emphases theirs).

Beyond dissemination and implementation, the effect that all of scientific inquiry has on altering clinical outcomes within a health system is unknown, not because the science may be flawed but because the gathering of unbiased information on clinical outcomes is fraught with difficulty. Very large scale trials approximate the conditions experienced in practice, but the number of such trials is limited; large scale databases have been used as indicators of outcomes, but they are constructed for administrative, not clinical purposes, and their validity has been questioned.[5] A recent publication, *Doing More Good Than Harm*,[6] contains cogent discussions of the value and limits of outcomes research. To date, there is little evidence that government policies have been greatly influenced by scientific inquiry, but the growing influence of health technology assessment holds promise, which could be extended to the organisation and management of services if greater investment were to be made in research on this topic.[7]

The cycle that we have described remains largely theoretical, because each step has not been formally validated. Indeed, it constitutes the core curriculum of health services research. The critical step in the whole process is implementation. All that precedes it is preparatory, and all that follows flows from its application.

The gap between research and practice

There is a range of examples of interventions for which unacceptable delays have occurred before their implementation, despite good evidence of their effectiveness. They include, for instance, the detection and management of hypertension,[8] [9] the appropriate management of women with breast cancer,[10] the eradication of *Helicobacter pylori* in patients with duodenal ulcer,[11] the use of thrombolytic therapy in patients with myocardial infarction,[12] [13] and the use of thromboprophylaxis after orthopaedic surgery.[14] There are also a number of examples in obstetrics including the use of the Cochrane database of perinatal trials, steroids in women in premature labour, and prophylactic antibiotics for women having caesarean sections.[15–17] At the same time interventions are still being used which are diagnostically and therapeutically ineffective such as dilatation and curettage for menstrual disorders in women under 40 years.[18] Finally, some interventions that have a considerable beneficial effect in certain groups of patients are being used more widely, including in groups of patients for whom there is no evidence of overall benefit—for example, the use of cholesterol lowering drugs in those at relatively low risk of ischaemic heart disease.[19]

The growing realisation of the gap between the output of research and clinical practice has led to increasing interest in methods to promote the uptake of research findings. There are several possible reasons for the gap between research and practice. These include the sheer volume of information in over 20 000 medical journals currently being published,[20] amounting to perhaps two million articles annually. The poor quality of many traditional review articles also contributes to the problem.[21] They have sometimes come to erroneous conclusions because, for instance, of selected inclusion of studies in the review or the failure of reviewers to understand that the lack of a positive result in individual studies does not imply lack of effectiveness if the statistical power is inadequate. Other factors that may mediate against the use of research findings by clinicians include the lack of skills to enable them critically to appraise the literature and the failure to link education programmes and clinical audit activities with the output of research. There may also be perverse incentives in health systems because health policy frequently does not take into account the need to promote effective practice. Hospitals, for instance, may receive payment according to the number of procedures that they undertake and not to their appropriateness. The failure of much health policy to be based on good evidence of effectiveness is a barrier to the promotion of clinical effectiveness as clinicians are hardly likely to accept one standard for themselves and another for managers and for government policy.

There is an extensive literature about the uptake of innovations both in health and non-health sectors.[22] While some of this literature tends to accept innovations uncritically this is not invariably the case. In medicine there have been a number of examples of inappropriate introductions of new technologies that have later been shown to be ineffective or even harmful including, for example, the postcoital test for infertility[23] or the use of lignocaine in the postinfarct patient.[12]

It is clear that the process of implementation is not merely a matter of transferring knowledge. It has been suggested, for instance, that the process has five steps starting with change in knowledge followed by persuasion which in turn depends on a number of characteristics of the innovation (figure 15.2). Research on different innovations in various sectors has suggested that those who acquire knowledge early in the process tend to have more extensive social networks, be more highly educated, and have higher social status than those who gain knowledge of the innovation at a later stage.[22] The perceived advantage is the degree to which the health professional considers the innovation to confer benefit to the patient(s) under consideration over and above alternative intervention(s). The complexity of an innovation is likely to determine its rate of uptake because of the implications for understanding and acquiring the skills to develop and use the innovation. This may be particularly important for organisational innovations in health care. Observability and trialability indicate the degree to which the innovation can be seen working and used on a limited or "one off" basis before its adoption, respectively. The magnitude of the importance of each of these factors is likely to vary according to the type of innovation. For example, in the case of organisational change such as the development of stroke units or home care services, trialability may be less relevant than observability because of the considerable resources required to set up such services.

Better quality information about clinical effectiveness is now becoming available in the form of systematic reviews and meta-analyses. These of course should not be accepted uncritically, but the methodology for undertaking and evaluating them has been developed.[24] The output of the Cochrane Collaboration and in the United Kingdom NHS reviews and dissemination centre is becoming more widely available and embracing an increasing range of.topics in the form of the Cochrane Reviews Database (available from the BMJ Publishing Group). Developments are

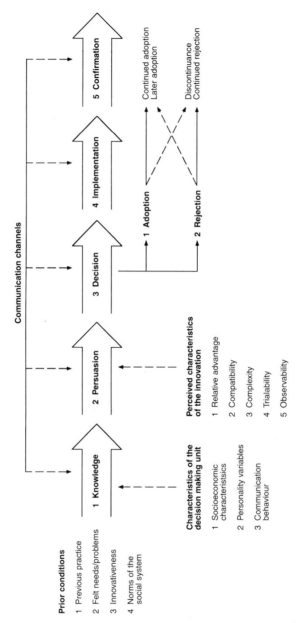

Figure 15.2 Model of the stages in the uptake of innovations. (Reprinted with the permission of The Free Press, an imprint of Simon & Schuster, from DIFFUSION OF INNOVATIONS, Third Edition by Everett M Rogers. Copyright 1962, 1971, 1983 by The Free Press).

now occurring in library services that could substantially improve the usefulness of medical literature to clinicians. These include clinical librarianship (involvement of the librarian as a member of the clinical team), training clinicians to search Medline, and quality filtering of information by the librarian.[25] In parallel with the development of improved evidence on clinical effectiveness there is a need for information about the effectiveness of interventions to promote the uptake of research findings. A Cochrane Collaboration group on effective professional practice has been set up to collate evidence based reviews on interventions to change the behaviour of health professionals. Examples of interventions to increase the uptake of research and development findings in the health sector are shown in the box.

A systematic review of trials of guideines showed that 81 of the 87 studies that examined effects on the process of care reported significant improvements as did 12 of 17 studies which assessed patient outcomes.[26] The reviewers concluded the guidelines were more likely to be effective if they took into account local circumstances and were disseminated by an active educational intervention. Patient specific reminders during a consultation can also enhance their effectiveness. A systematic review of the continuing medical education (CME) strategies found 99 trials containing 160 interventions. Nearly two thirds resulted in an improvement in at least one major outcome measure. Effective strategies included reminders, patient mediated interventions, outreach visits, and multifaceted activities. Formal CME conferences or activities without enabling or practice reinforcing strategies had little impact.[27] A systematic review of computerised decision support systems showed that there were 28 randomised trials and, although only a minority were aimed at promoting more effective treatment, there was considerable evidence that they could have an impact.[28] Another review has identified studies of social influence approaches such as the use of opinion leaders, change agents, and academic detailing (the latter being defined as face to face transmission of information to health professionals by trained individuals with the opportunity to discuss the implications). Further information is needed on the cost effectiveness and generalisability of social influence approaches. For instance there are few studies on opinion leaders, and these have given varying results. (J Grimshaw et al, personal communication). It is clear from studies in the United States that academic detailing can have an impact in some environments.[29] [30] An early review of audit and feedback

145

Factors that may influence the implementation of research findings in the NHS[34]

Characteristics of message (research findings) including
- Scientific quality
- Source
- Content (complexity of information)
- Presentation (for example, relative vs absolute risk reduction; numbers needed to treat; individual studies vs systematic reviews)

Characteristics of players (those influencing practice or being influenced) including combinations of
- Individual health professionals and managers
- Purchasing organisations
- Provider organisations (trusts and health authorities, including non-executive directors)
- Professional organisations (including royal colleges)
- Industry—for example, pharmaceutical
- Education providers
- Research information providers
- Researchers
- Public
- Patients
- User groups
- Media
- "Alliance" partners—for example, local authorities
- Policy makers

Characteristics of interventions including combinations of
- Use of clinical guidelines
- Audit and feedback
- Conferences
- Local consensus processes
- Educational approaches
- Marketing
- Opinion leaders
- Reminders/computerised decison support
- Patient mediated interventions

Levers, facilitators, and barriers including combinations of
- Availability of resources
- Availability of time
- Financial/contractual
- Statute
- Professional incentives/disincentives
- Cultural/social/organisational norms

suggested that such interventions can be effective in modifying professional behaviour, but there are some unanswered questions such as how and to whom the feedback should be given—for example, immediate to the individual clinician or delayed to groups.[31] The systematic review of CME strategies found audit and feedback a relatively less effective approach than other enabling and reinforcing strategies,[27] and more work is clearly needed. As part of the United Kingdom NHS research and development programme an advisory group was convened to decide on priorities for evaluation of methods for implementation. The group identified a number of barriers and levers as well as key players which could influence the implementation process. After a national consultation process it identified 20 priority areas in which further research is now being commissioned.[32] Four types

---

Priority areas for evaluation[34]

Research into the following is suggested

- The influence of source and presentation of evidence on its uptake by health care professionals and others
- The principal sources of information on health care effectiveness used by clinicians
- The management of uncertainty and communication of risk by clinicians
- Roles for health service users in implementing research
- Why some clinicians but not others change their practice in response to research findings
- The role of commissioning in securing change in clinical practice
- Professional, managerial, organisational, and commercial factors associated with securing change in clinical practice, with a particular focus on trusts and primary care providers
- Interventions directed at clinical and medical directors and directors of nursing in trusts to promote evidence based care
- Local research implementation and development projects (such as GRiPP)
- Effectiveness and cost effectiveness of audit and feedback to promote implementation of research findings
- Educational strategies for continuing professional development to promote the implementation of research findings
- Effectiveness and cost effectiveness of teaching critical appraisal skills to clinicians, patients/users, purchasers, and providers to promote uptake of research findings
- The role of undergraduate (prequalification) training in promoting the uptake of research findings
- The impact of clinical practice guidelines in disciplines other than medicine
- Effectiveness and cost effectiveness of reminder and decision support systems to implement research findings
- The role of the media in promoting uptake of research findings
- Impact of professional and managerial change agents (including educational outreach visits) and local opinion leaders in implementing research findings
- Effect on evidence based practice of general health policy measures
- The impact of national guidance to promote clinical effectiveness
- The use of research based evidence by policy makers

---

of studies were deemed necessary, which varied according to the priority area: systematic reviews, descriptive and hypothesis generating studies, phase 1 intervention studies (examining the feasibility, acceptability, and potential generalisability of local implementation projects), and phase 2 intervention studies (rigorously designed, generally multicentre, intervention trials). It is envisaged that the projects commissioned as part of this programme will influence the way in which implementation strategies are designed and undertaken in the United Kingdom and hopefully elsewhere.

There is no doubt that the continuing advances in scientific knowledge have posed considerable challenges for the practice of medicine and the organisation of health care. It is clearly vital that the methods used to promote effective practice are themselves of demonstrable effectiveness. At the same time public opinion and the views of individual patients and their families will also be crucial in determining patterns of care. It is therefore essential that activities to promote effective practice involve not only practitioners themselves but also managers, policy makers, and the wider public, particularly through user groups who may be concerned with a specific condition, category of disease, or group within the population. The development of a more integrated system of change management in which all the key players are involved will necessitate breaking down barriers between those engaged in education of health professionals, quality and clinical audit, research and development, and health policy,[33] who in the past have all too often functioned independently of each other.

1 House of Lords Select Committee on Science and Technology. *Medical research and the NHS reforms.* London: HMSO, 1995.
2 Department of Health. *Research and development: towards an evidence based health service.* London: DoH, 1995.
3 Halvorsen KT. Combining results from independent investigations: meta-analysis in medical research. In: Bailer JC III, Mosteller F, eds. *Medical uses of statistics.* Waltham, Massachusetts: NEJM Books, 1986: 392–416.
4 Radical Statistics Health group. NHS "indicators of success": what do they tell us? *BMJ* 1995; **310**: 1045–50.
5 Sheldon TA. Please bypass the PORT: observational studies of effectiveness run a poor second to randomised controlled trials. *BMJ* 1994; **309**: 142–5.
6 Warren KS, Mosteller F, eds. Doing more good than harm; the evaluation of health care interventions. *Ann NY Acad Sci* 1993; **703**: 1–341.
7 Haines A, Iliffe S. Innovations in services and the appliance of science. *BMJ* 1995: **310**; 815–6.
8 Smith WCS, Lee AJ, Crombie IK, *et al.* Control of blood pressure in Scotland: the rule of halves. *BMJ* 1990; **300**: 981–3.
9 Kurji KH, Haines A. Detection and management of hypertension in general practice in north west London. *BMJ* 1984; **288**: 903–5.

10 Chouillet AM, Bell CMJ, Hiscox JG. Management of breast cancer in southeast England. *BMJ* 1994, **308**: 168–71.
11 Moore RA. Helicobacter pylori and peptic ulcer. Oxford: Health Technology Evaluation Association, 1995.
12 Antman E, Lau J, Kupelnick B, *et al.* A comparison of the results of meta-analysis of randomised controlled trials and recommendations of clinical experts. *JAMA* 1992; **268**: 240–8.
13 Ketley D, Woods KL. Impact of clinical trials on clinical practice: example of the thrombolysis for acute myocardial infarction. *Lancet* 1993: **342**: 891–4.
14 Laverick MD, Croal SA, Mollan RAB. Orthopaedic surgeons and thromboprophylaxis. *BMJ* 1991; **303**: 549–50.
15 Patterson-Brown S, Wyatt J, Fisk NM. Are clinicians interested in up to date reviews of effective care? *BMJ* 1993; **307**: 1464.
16 Donaldson L. Maintaining excellence. *BMJ* 1992; **305**: 1280–4.
17 Chalmers I. Improving the quality and dissemination of reviews of clinical research. In: Lock S, ed. *The future of medical journals.* London: BMJ Publishing Group, 1991: 127–46.
18 Coulter A, Klassen A, MacKenzie I, *et al.* Diagnostic dilation and currettage: is it used appropriately? *BMJ* 1993; **306**: 236–9.
19 Davey-Smith G, Song F, Sheldon TA. Cholesterol lowering and mortality: the importance of considering initial level of risk. *BMJ* 1993; **306**: 1367–73.
20 Mulrow CD. Rationale for systematic reviews. *BMJ* 1994; **309**: 597–9.
21 Mulrow CD. The medical review article; state of the science. *Ann Intern Med* 1987; **104**: 470–1.
22 Rogers EM. *The diffusion of innovations.* New York: Free Press, 1983.
23 Grimes DA. Technology follies. *JAMA* 1993; **269**: 3030–3.
24 Oxman A, Chalmers I, Clarke M, *et al*, eds. *Cochrane collaboration handbook, section VI: preparing and maintaining systematic reviews.* Oxford: Cochrane Collaboration, 1994.
25 Nuffield Institute for Health, University of Leeds, Centre for Health Economics and the NHS Centre for Reviews and Dissemination, University of York, Research Unit Royal College of Physicians. *Implementing clinical practice guidelines* Dec 1994, No. 8. p. 11.
26 Marshall JG. Issues in clinical information delivery. *Library Trends* 1993, **42**; 83–107.
27 Davis DA, Thomson MA, Oxman AD, *et al.* Changing physician performance, a systematic review of the effect of continuing medical strategies. *JAMA* 1995; **274**: 700–5.
28 Johnston ME. Langton KB, Haynes RB, *et al.* The effects of computer based clinical decision support systems on clinician performance and patients outcome. A critical appraisal of research. *Ann Intern Med* 1994; **120**: 135–42.
29 Avorn J, Soumerai S. Improving drug therapy decisions through educational outreach. *N Engl J Med* 1983; **308**: 1457–63.
30 Soumerai S, Avorn J. Principles of educational outreach ('academic detailing') to improve clinical decision making. *JAMA* 1990; **263**: 549–56.
31 Mugford M, Banfield P, O'Hanlon M. Effects of feedback of information on clinical practice: a review. *BMJ* 1991; **303**: 398–402.
32 Advisory Group to the Central Research and Development Committee. *Priorities for the evaluation of methods of implementation of research findings.* London: Department of Health, 1995.
33 Haines A, Jones R. Implementing findings of research. *BMJ* 1994; **308**: 1488–92.

16 Theory and practice of economic appraisal in health care

FRANS RUTTEN

As the impact of economic appraisal on health policy and medical practice is growing the discussion on methodological and practical issues is getting more intense. This is, for instance, reflected in the publication of the various guidelines on economic appraisal in Australia, Canada, Ontario, the United Kingdom, Italy, and various other European countries. Also initiatives of the scientific community can be reported, such as the cost effectiveness panel on clinical and preventive services under the chairmanship of Milton Weinstein and the European Commission funded concerted action on the harmonisation by consensus of the methodology for economic evaluation of health technologies in the European Union. Jacobs *et al* recently compared the most prominent of the existing guidelines for the conduct of economic evaluations and suggested that differences can be related to differences in the purposes for which the guidelines have been drawn up.[1] One could add that the formal place of economic appraisal in the decision making process also makes a difference: it is understandable that the Australian authorities do not wish to consider other costs than those related to the drugs budget, while the British guidelines, which are not formally linked to policy making, can afford a more flexible stance in this matter.

Although there seems to be consensus on the basic principles and concepts in economic appraisal, I would like to pinpoint a few areas where there is still methodological debate. These are the theoretical foundation of economic appraisal, outcome measurement, and costing. I will cover the controversial issues and make observations on the practical application of economic appraisal.

150

The theoretical foundation of economic appraisal

Economic appraisal sets out to answer the question of whether a number of interventions—A, B, C, etc—should be undertaken and, if investable funds are limited, which one, two, or more should be selected. In welfare theory those projects should be selected that make society as a whole better off, or in other words, lead to a potential Pareto improvement. This means that the project is capable of producing an excess of benefits such that everyone in society could, by a costless redistribution of gains, be made better off. In welfare theory the values that individuals place on the outcomes of an intervention are decisive. This in accordance with a cost-benefit approach, where the benefits of an intervention are, for instance, measured in terms of the willingness of individuals to pay for these outcomes. But it is in conflict with the implicit assumptions of cost effectiveness analysis and cost utility analysis, where the outcomes of an intervention are measured in some natural unit or QALY concept chosen by the analyst. Mishan points out that such cost effectiveness analysis may show that intervention A is more efficient than intervention B in reaching a particular objective, but that even the most cost effective strategy should not be recommended when the societal costs exceed the value that society would place on the associated benefits.[2] So cost effectiveness would allow only the selection of strategies from a narrow perspective. Several authors have pointed to the related problems of using cost effectiveness league tables in health care policy.[3-5]

If cost-benefit analysis is the superior approach why do we see so little of it? In practice it is difficult to find an acceptable way of putting a money value on QALYs or other measures so that their value can be compared directly with that of the costs. If health care services were traded in competitive markets such value could be derived from the demand curve as observed in such markets. As health care is often not traded on competitive markets this observation is not of much help. The main alternative to using revealed preference is the direct estimation of people's willingness to pay for health gains by way of questionnaires containing contingent valuation questions. Such questions can be raised in the form of a so called bidding game, where the respondent is asked to accept or reject a sequence of bids until his or her maximum willingness to pay is reached. The problem with such an approach is the emergence of a starting point bias. The alternative, a binary contingent valuation questionnaire, requires a large number of respondents and a stratification of respondents in such samples as each individual response provides little information. There is some consensus now to use binary rather than open ended contingent valuation questions,[6] but the approach is still used in only a few actual studies.

Cost effectiveness or rather cost utility analysis is the dominant approach at the moment, and this can be defended on the grounds that if QALYs are based on uniform and generally applicable concepts a cost utility analysis is appropriate for determining priorities within a public budget targeted at maximising health gains and that only a monetary value for a QALY is required to bridge the gap towards a cost-benefit analysis. This is all under the assumption that a societal perspective is the relevant one. Of course, other perspectives—for example, for a particular health care organisation—may also be relevant for supporting decision making within such an organisation. For such more narrow perspectives cost effectiveness analysis or cost utility analysis or even cost minimisation analysis may suffice.

Outcome measurement

With respect to outcome measurement I would like to concentrate on the use of QALYs. Most authors would agree that QALYs should represent individual preferences rather than some decision maker's perspective. The first question then is whether QALYs, measured principally through three methods (rating scale, time trade off, and standard gamble) represent a valid description of actual preferences of individuals.Bleichrodt has shown that for QALYs to be a valid representation of individual preferences it suffices to impose risk neutrality for life years in every health state.[7] This means that the individual is indifferent between a lottery over life years and the expected life duration of that lottery. Many empirical studies, however, have rejected this assumption on preference behaviour. Another model proposed for describing preferences is that using the healthy years equivalents.[8] HYEs were claimed to require no assumptions about the form of the person's utility function and thus to reflect individual preferences better, but this has been challenged. If the constant proportional trade off assumption holds HYEs and QALYs measured through time trade off will be identical.[9] The constant proportional trade off assumption states that the proportion of remaining life that one would be willing to trade for a specified quality improvement is independent of the amount of the remaining life. Recent work suggested that this assumption could not be rejected.[10] We conclude that HYEs do not offer additional advantages in describing individual preferences but are definitely more difficult to calculate.

If we accept that QALYs are the best measure in cost utility analysis until now, there is also debate on what would be the best way to measure the quality weights to construct QALYs. There is some theoretical ground to prefer time trade off and standard gamble above the rating scale method, but there is little empirical evidence for the superiority of one over the others. Recently Bleichrodt used a student population to examine the ability of the three methods to rank health profiles.[7] This study indicated the time trade off may be the preferred method. Utility measurement through one of the three methods in actual studies is rarely performed. In many cases generic questionnaires on health status are used to describe outcomes in various dimensions of health and then multi-attribute utility functions are used to estimate the quality weights. This is done, for instance, when the EuroQol questionnaire is applied and when a model to construct utility values from the outcomes generated by the questionnaire is used. The quality weights in such models should of course have been validated against the time trade off method or the standard gamble method. Research is currently under way to validate the existing models to generate utility values for the EuroQol and to extend the empirical basis for these models. Similar exercises are planned for other generic health questionnaires, such as the SF-36.

To conclude, we observe consensus in the literature about the use of QALYs, but more research is necessary to show that QALYs validly reflect preference choices of individuals.

Costing

With respect to costing the Batelle Medical Technology Assessment and Policy Research Centre stated in 1993 that there seems to be consensus on how direct costs should be treated, but that there is probably less conformity in actual studies in terms of how costs are treated.[11] It was further suggested that the opposite seems to be true of indirect costs, where standard approaches like the human capital are used empirically, but there is no consensus on how they should be used. If the topics of controversy with respect to direct costing are considered there is the question how to value time lost to the patient and his of her family apart from productivity losses. Such valuation of time lost may be partly picked up on the benefit side by a sensitive health related quality of life instrument, but also on the cost side there may be cases of lost time representing real lost resources and thus real costs. How to value lost time depends on the person's circumstances and on his or her employment. The same goes for the time of the supplier of informal care. Smith and Wright have shown that time input for informal care may even have a positive value for the care giver.[12]

Another issue in direct costing is how to deal with transfer payments. The current guidelines for economic appraisal suggest that all transfer payments should be excluded from the cost figures as these do not represent time resource costs but merely a redistribution of wealth. As far as income taxes and social security premiums are concerned one may argue that production factors can be deployed in a health programme only if you pay the gross market costs. Employees for instance may consider their social security rights as preferences without which they would not be willing to give their labour input. This suggests that social premiums are linked to production factors that should be taken into account when determining prices. This is not true for indirect taxes (for example, value added tax) as they do not play a part in deciding about the deployment of production factors. This position to include direct taxes and social premiums but to exclude indirect taxes would support what is being done in most studies.

A final issue regarding direct costing is that of marginal versus average costs. In my opinion the question to choose depends on the context of the policy decision that is being supported by the economic analysis. If the study has to support a decision of a hospital manager clearly the marginal costs of the various options in this specific hospital are the relevant cost items. If it is a matter of national policy average costs may be more appropriate as these reflect the true variable costs when the volume of services is high and the services are well diffused across the country. Furthermore, little attention has been given to analysis of whether savings, which are reported to occur as a consequence of health care intervention, are actually fully recouped and what time path is associated with recoupment of these savings. Clearly, this depends among other things on the incentives facing various participants in the health care system.

Indirect costs as a consequence of loss of productivity may constitute a substantial part of estimated costs or savings in economic evaluations of health care programmes. The existing guidelines on the conduct of economic appraisal take different positions regarding the inclusion of indirect costs in economic appraisals. Hesitation to include indirect costs, as exists both with analysts and policy makers, is mostly generated by the fact that these costs have consistently been overestimated by using the human capital approach in a straightforward manner. As I have shown elsewhere indirect costs may be reduced by a factor of 10 when one takes into account the effect that after adaptation absent workers generally can be replaced at some costs, given unemployment, both registered and hidden, above the friction level.[13] [14] Table 16.1 shows the indirect costs of disease in the Netherlands for 1988 by using the human capital approach and the so called friction cost approach. The basic idea of the friction cost method is that the amount of production lost due to disease depends on the time span organisations need to restore the initial production level. Production losses are assumed to be confined to the period needed to replace a sick worker, called the friction period. In the Dutch study long term indirect costs, associated with absence from work and incidence of disability, were estimated with a macroeconometric sectoral model for the Netherlands with another 0.8% added to the total indirect costs of disease.

Table 16.1 Indirect costs (% of net national income) of disease in the Netherlands for 1988 in billions of guilders[14]

Cost category	Friction costs-1988	Human capital costs-1988
Absence from work	9.2	23.8
Disability	0.15	49.1
Mortality	0.15	8.0
Total indirect costs	9.5 (2.1%)	80.9 (18%)

This friction cost method accommodates several critical remarks made about the human capital approach[15-18] and meets a number of the suggestions made in the Australian and Canadian guidelines. There has not been much debate yet on this friction cost method, but we may draw some preliminary conclusions. Given the relevance of indirect costs it seems preferable to insist that they are estimated as realistically as possible instead of estimating the potential economic consequences of disease in an

155

exceptional state of full employment when the human capital approach is used. In estimating indirect costs the following issues should be analysed further:

- The short term impact of absence from work on production and costs
- The time span during which production and costs are affected directly, depending on the situation within the firm as well as on the labour market
- The long term indirect costs of absence from work and disability.

Further study is needed on the extent of production losses that may occur during illness without absence from work. Absence of indirect costs should incorporate production loss in relation to unpaid labour to prevent adverse equity implications, but data on work absence and disability related to unpaid labour are extremely scarce. The exact consequences of short term absence from work for labour productivity and costs need to be analysed in more detail on the level of the firm. We have shown that indirect costs are important when health care programmes bring forth health effects in the short run, when there is a major impact on (short term) absence from work, and if a considerable proportion of the target population is employed at the time they receive the benefits of the programme.[13] Unless it can be demonstrated that their importance is negligible, indirect costs are to be included in baseline estimates of costs in economic evaluations.

Remaining issues

The most important other issues, where there is still little agreement, are the choice of a discount rate, how to deal with uncertainty in economic appraisal, and the proper incorporation of considerations of equity. Most economists would agree that health outcomes and monetary costs should be discounted, but there is considerable diagreement about the appropriate discount rate. And some researchers would even favour a zero discount rate for non-monetary outcomes. Time preference theory and the concept of opportunity cost of capital are both used as an argument for discounting costs, the former being related to individual preferences and the latter being concerned with efficiency in resource allocation. As non-monetary outcomes cannot be traded over time the opportunity costs argument does not apply to discounting benefits.[19] As the relation between costs of medical treatment and benefits gained may change considerably over time one may even want to apply a variable discount rate rather than a constant one. In practice we see some general agreement to use 5% or 6% discount rate for both costs and benefits, but this procedure is not supported by theory or by empirical evidence.

Some work can now be reported on the systematic and comprehensive consideration of uncertainty in economic appraisal.[20] [21] When both costs and effects are observed in a clinical trial the data can be used to construct confidence intervals surrounding the cost effectiveness ratios through a rather complex procedure. Further development and operationalisation of methods is necessary to make this approach commonly used.

And, finally, there is very little work done on the incorporation of equity considerations in economic evaluation studies. Bleichrodt has identified a number of conditions underlying the unweighted aggregation of QALYs over individuals.[7] Relaxing some of these conditions he proposed algorithms allowing a trade off between the efficiency gains of a health care programme against its adverse equity implications.

Practical application

Growing consensus on methodological issues in economic appraisal does not automatically translate into better quality of applied research. Many authors have observed a clear growth in the economic evaluative literature, some of whom had specific reservations about the quality of some work.[22-26] Some of these worries used to originate from observing methodological mistakes, but more recently there is more concern about the use of proper sources of information, about the extrapolation from observations made in a limited context (for example, a clinical trial), and about the discretionary use of information in modelling exercises.[27] This concern is, for instance, reflected in the new version of the Australian guidelines,[28] which impose stricter rules on the use of certain sources of information and emphasise the importance of using uniform cost figures. The latter is stimulated in Australia by the publication of a manual of resource items and their associated costs by the Commonwealth Department of Health, Housing, Local Government, and Community Services. Furthermore, the place of modelling in economic appraisal is stipulated as helpful in dealing with limitations of randomised evidence as the preferred basis for economic appraisal. More specifically modelling is suggested to help in linking surrogate outcomes to final outcomes; to extrapolate the outcomes measured beyond the duration of the trial; to examine the impact of differences between the eligibility criteria and settings of the trial and conditions in actual practice; to modify patterns of use of resources measured in one country to reflect those in another country; and, finally, to include resource consumption not measured in a trial and to exclude consumption of resources driven by protocol.

Conclusions

In conclusion, we see two developments that may counteract as regards the quality of research in this area. One is that there is growing concern on methodological standards but also much progress in reaching consensus on how to deal with the few remaining methodological controversies. The other trend is the growing demand for cost effectiveness information, which an increasing number of players on the supply side are trying to meet. Commercialisation in research holds the danger that economic appraisal loses its scientific endeavour. Through education of all participants in health care and through improving the quality of peer review processes we may observe a steady growth of research work in the future, not only in quantitive but also in qualitative sense.

1 Jacobs P, Bachynsky J, Baladi JF. A comparative review of pharmacoeconomic guidelines. *PharmacoEconomics* 1995; **8**: 182–9.
2 Mishan EJ. *Cost-benefit analysis*. 4th ed. London: Unwin Hyman, 1988.
3 Birch S, Gafni A. Cost-effectiveness/utility analysed. Do current decision rules lead us to where we want to be? *Journal of Health Economics* 1992; **11**: 279–96.
4 Drummond M, Torrance G, Mason J. Cost-effectiveness league tables: more harm than good? *Soc Sci Medi* 1993; **37**: 33–40.
5 Birch S, Gafni A. Cost-effectiveness ratios: in a league of their own. *Health Policy* 1994; **28**: 133–41.
6 National Oceanic and Atmospheric Administration. Report of the NOAA-panel on contingent valuation. *Federal Register* 1993; **58**: 4602–14.
7 Bleichrodt H. *Applications of utility theory in economic evaluation of health care*, Rotterdam: Erasmus University, 1996. (PhD dissertation).
8 Mehrez A, Gafni A. Quality-adjusted life-years, utility theory and healthy-years equivalents. *Med Decis Making* 1989; **9**: 142–9.
9 Culyer AJ, Wagstaff A. QALYs versus HYEs. *Journal of Health Economics* 1993; **12**: 311–23.
10 Bleichrodt H, Johannesson M. An experimental test of constant proportional trade-off and utility independence. *Med Decis Making* (in press).
11 Batelle (Medtap), *Methods of cost-effectiveness analysis: areas of consensus and debate*. Washington DC; Medtap, 1993.
12 Smith K, Wright K. Informal care and economic appraisal: a discussion of possible methodological approaches. *Health Econ* 1994; **3**: 137–48.

13 Koopmanschap MA, Rutten FFH. The impact of indirect costs on outcomes of health care programmes. *Health Econ* 1994, **13**: 385–93.

14 Koopmanschap MA, Rutten FFH, Ineveld BM van, *et al.* The friction cost method for measuring indirect costs of disease. *Journal of Health Economics* 1995; **14**: 171–89.

15 Drummond M, Cost-of-illness studies: a major headache? *PharmacoEconomics* 1992; **2**: 1–4.

16 Gerard K, Donaldson C, Maynard AK. The cost of diabetes. *Diabet Med* 1989; **6**: 164–70.

17 Lindgren B. *Costs of illness in Sweden 1964–1975*. Lund, Sweden: Liber, 1981.

18 Williams A. Economics of coronary artery bypass grafting. *BMJ* 1985; **291**: 326–9.

19 Hillman AL, Kim MS, Economic decision making in health care; a standard approach to discounting health outcomes. *PharmacoEconomics* 1995; **7**: 198–205.

20 O'Brien BJ, Drummond MF. Statistical versus quantitative significance in the socio-economic evaluation of medicines, *PharmacoEconomics* 1994; **5**: 389–98.

21 Hout BA van, AL MJ, Gordon GS, Rutten FFH. Costs, effects and c/e ratios alongside clinical trial. *Health Econ* 1994; **3**: 309–19.

22 Drummond MF. *Studies in economic appraisal*. Oxford: Oxford University Press, 1981.

23 Drummond MF, Ludbrook A, Lowson K, *et al. Studies in economic appraisal in health care*. Vol 2. Oxford: Oxford University Press, 1986.

24 Udvarhelhi IS, Colditz GA, Epstein AM. Cost-effectiveness and cost-benefit analysis in the medical literature. Are methods being used correctly? *Ann Intern Med* 1992; **166**: 238–44.

25 Gerard K. *A review of cost-utility studies: assessing their policy-making relevance.* Aberdeen: University of Aberdeen, 1991. (HERU Discussion Paper 11/91.)

26 Backhouse ME, Backhouse RJ, Edey SA. Economic evaluation bibliography, *Health Econ* 1992; **1** suppl: 1–235.

27 Kassirer JD, Angell M. The journal's policy on cost-effectiveness analyses. *N Engl J Med* 1994; **331**: 669–70.

28 Commonwealth Government. *Draft guidelines for the pharmaceutical industry on preparation of submissions to the PBAC; including submissions involving economic analyses.* Canberra; Commonwealth Government, 1995.

17 Monitoring and evaluating a community based mental health service: the epidemiological approach

MICHELE TANSELLA, MIRELLA RUGGERI

In most countries mental health services are undergoing substantial changes, a common element of the change being the transition from a system of care predominantly hospital based to one that is mainly community based. Monitoring and evaluating are essential elements for making the delivery of care more rational, especially during a transition phase in the organisation of services and in the provision of psychiatric care. A continuous cycle of planning and evaluation is necessary and both should have, whenever possible, an epidemiological basis.[1]

Monitoring is the first step in the evaluative process. It needs to be carried out in an accurate and reliable way and for a sufficiently long period of time. It is widely recognised that the most accurate way of estimating the uptake of psychiatric care by a target population is provided by psychiatric case registers. They have two main advantages:

- They permit patient centred longitudinal registrations of contacts with a wide, sometimes overlapping, set of specialised services
- They provide epidemiological based information that facilitates comparisons over time between areas and within the same area.

On the other hand, evaluation should be developed as a further step after monitoring and should concern a representative sample of all patients actually in contact with the psychiatric services to be evaluated. There are now available several technologies, instruments, and methodologies to evaluate a mental health service.[2]

The aim of this chapter is to give some examples of monitoring and evaluating a community based mental health service. Such a service has been defined as "a comprehensive and well integrated system of care devoted to a defined population, which includes a wide spectrum of outpatient, day patient, and general hospital inpatient facilities, as well as staffed and unstaffed residential facilities. It should ensure easy access of patients to any of its components, early diagnosis, continuity of care as well as social support and close liaison with other community medical and social services, in particular with general practitioners".[3] We will report on data collected in the South Verona community psychiatric service, which has operated since 1978 and was established under the provision of the Italian psychiatric reform.[4]

Monitoring a community based mental health service

Monitoring consists mainly of a regular and continuous recording of all contacts made by patients with a defined set of services and facilities. These service data may be aggregated in several ways. Potentially useful methods of aggregation include aggregation by unit of time (for example, visits a year), by specific source of services (for example, visits to an outpatient department), by type of sector (for example, admissions to all outpatient facilities or admissions to all inpatient units), by type of care provided (for example, visits made by psychiatrists), by episode of illness (for example, visits during the time interval between the onset or recurrence of an episode of depression and its resolution), and by episodes of care (for example, contacts made during a specified period of time, such as one year, with a series of psychiatric services). The episode is the most conceptually useful method of aggregating data on mental health services. It is worth noting, however, that episodes of illness are based on the mental health of the individual patient, whereas episodes of care are based on patterns of use of service during a fixed period of time.[5] Research into mental health services with the latter method of aggregating service data is most useful when epidemiologically based—that is, when it concerns patients living in a geographically defined area and may be conducted only in areas where a psychiatric case register is operating.[6]

Long term monitoring of psychiatric care in South Verona

South Verona is mainly urban, relatively affluent, and predominantly middle class with a low migration rate. The total population is about 75 000 inhabitants. The South Verona community psychiatric service, which was established in 1978 and developed gradually over the past 18 years, is the main psychiatric service that provides care to the South Verona residents. It includes a comprehensive and well integrated number of programmes and provides inpatient care, day care, rehabilitation, outpatient care, and home visits as well as a 24 hour emergency service and residential facilities (three apartments and one hostel) for long term patients.

A psychiatric case register, which covers the same geographical area of the South Verona community psychiatric service, started on 31 December 1978 and has been operating since. Private hospitals and other agencies in the larger province of Verona also provide information to the psychiatric case register. Data for 1990–3, however, indicate that 81.8% of patients living in the area are receiving care from the South Verona community psychiatric service alone (79.2%) or by the service together with other services (2.6%). Deaths and moves to outside the area are checked and recorded yearly in the psychiatric case register. Sociodemographic information and psychiatric history (21 items) are collected at first contact and routinely updated directly by the professionals concerned (including nurses) and checked by the register staff. All extramural contacts are classified as "booked" or "drop in". Length of each extramural contact (number of minutes) is also routinely recorded. Diagnoses of all new cases are reviewed by the register's director (MT) using the *International Classification of Diseases*.[7]

The South Verona register is used for clinical, administrative, and research purposes. Among the clinical uses we should mention the provision to the clinical teams of lists of severely mentally ill patients who have been in contact and are to be reassessed at regular intervals to ensure better continuity of care and to improve practices. For producing these lists working definitions of severely mentally ill are reached pragmatically and suggested to the register staff by the clinicians concerned. For this purpose a combination of several variables, such as the diagnosis, the number of hospital admissions, the number of episodes of illness, the total number of contacts over a specified period of time, the occupational status, the concomitant physical illnesses, the contacts with many (for example, more than three) psychiatric agencies, etc, is considered. Another clinical use concerns the follow up of individual patients: a complete description of the amount of care received by all institutions and services reporting to the register may be provided to clinicians on request.

Administrative uses of the register include the provision of prevalence figures, incidence rates, number of patients seen, and number of visits made over different periods of time. The register is also used for monitoring the effects of changes in resources, organisation, needs, etc, over time and as a basis for calculating direct costs.[8 9]

As reported above, in mental health service research the study of episodes of care over time and in relation to changes in service provision and organisation is particularly useful. The register has been used to complete longitudinal studies of patterns of care and episodes of care designed for assessing continuity of care for patients with chronic and severe mental illnesses by using methods of "survival analysis".[6 10 11] Other research uses include the use of the register as a sampling frame for studies on specific groups of patients[12-14]; comparative studies on the uses of services in different geographical areas[5-18]; studies on the association between social deprivation and use of psychiatric services[19 20]; and long term studies on mortality among psychiatric patients.[21] Figure 17.1 shows the patterns of care in South Verona from 1979 till 1994. It may be seen that since 1979 hospital care has been consistently decreasing whereas outpatient and community care have been steadily increasing. These changes over time demonstrate that community care needs adequate time to be implemented and that after 15 years the situation is not yet stable and the number of contacts in the community is still increasing.

Inpatient psychiatric admissions before and after the 1978 psychiatric reform have also been monitored. In 1994 as compared with 1977 there was a 22% decrease of inpatient admissions with a 89% decrease in compulsory admissions, a complete halt of new admissions to state mental hospitals, an increase in the use of beds in the public sector, and a decrease in the use of beds in private hospitals. The mean number of occupied

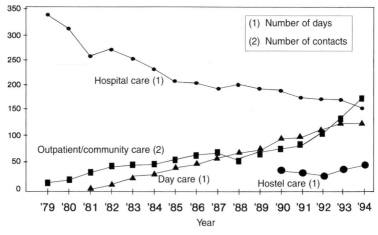

Figure 17.1 Patterns of care in psychiatric patients in South Verona (ratios per 1000 adults).

beds per day also consistently decreased over time and in 1994 was 59% lower than in 1979 (see table 17.1). This decrease is entirely due to the reduced number of patients remaining in the state mental hospital. Since admissions to state mental hospital ceased in 1981 this reduction can be expected to continue for the next decade. In 1994 the number of beds occupied in both public and private hospitals was 0.25 per 1000 at risk, and this figure has been constant for some years.

Since 1979 the numbers of long stay patients (those who stay in hospital continuously for one year or more) are consistently decreasing whereas the numbers of long term patients (those not long stay patients who are continuously in contact, for one year or

Table 17.1 Mean occupied beds/day before (1977) and after the psychiatric reform (per 100 000 adult residents of South Verona).

Type of care	1977	1979	1982	1985	1988	1991	1994	Difference
In state mental hospitals	86	69	43	32	30	25	18	−79%
In other public hospitals	9	16	14	17	19	16	15	+67%
In private hospitals	9	7	10	7	6	7	10	+11%
Total	104	93	67	57	55	48	43	−59%

more, with some psychiatric service, not necessarily the same service or only one service, with a gap between two contacts never longer than 90 days) are steadily increasing.

Evaluating a community based mental health service

In the past, rates of morbidity and mortality or data on service utilisation have been used as main indicators of outcome. The assessment of outcome of psychiatric care, especially when provided by community based services, should also include measures such as quality of life, unmet needs, and satisfaction with services.[22-26] Moreover, evaluative studies of the cost effectiveness of community based psychiatric services should integrate quantitive and qualitative variables and should consider various domains (that is, being multidimensional) and different perspectives (that is, being multiaxial).[26-30]

Though the monitoring of psychiatric care provided to the South Verona residents started almost at the same time as the implementation of the new system of care, the evaluative studies started later on. Firstly, we completed a few investigations to evaluate the outcome of care in selected groups of patients for example, patients with a diagnosis of schizophrenia[13 14]; then as already mentioned, we compared community based psychiatric care in South Verona and in areas with different social and demographic characteristics.

The South Verona outcome project

In the past few years we have developed an integrated model for assessing the outcome of care routinely: the South Verona outcome project (OUT-*pro*). According to this model variables belonging to four main dimensions are considered: clinical variables, social variables, variables concerning the interaction with services (specifically, needs for care, satisfaction with services, family burden), and data on service utilisation and costs. Both quantitive and qualitative measures are used, and the assessment for the latter is multiaxial—that is, takes into account the perspectives of patients, relatives, and professionals.

The project is an attempt to standardise information that clinicians collect and record in periodical reviews of cases in treatment and in their everyday clinical practice and to employ for service evaluation the same professionals concerned in the clinical work. Most of the assessments are actually completed, after a short training, by the clinicians themselves, some other assessments are made by the patients, with the help of research workers. The aims of the South Verona outcome project are:

- To study the outcome of community care by using a naturalistic and longitudinal approach in evaluating outcome
- To identify topics of interest for experimental studies
- To promote standardisation of routine clinical assessments— that is, to improve the quality of the clinical records.

Standardised assessments take place twice a year: from April to June (wave A) and from October to December (wave B). During these periods both first ever patients and patients already in contact with the service are assessed at the first or, at the latest, the second time they are seen. In wave A the assessment in made only by the key professional (in most cases a psychiatrist or a psychologist) and includes the global assessment of functioning scale (GAF),[31] the brief psychiatric rating scale "expanded version" (BPRS),[32] eight items from the disability assessment scale (DAS-II),[33] and the Camberwell assessment of needs (CAN) (M Phelan, M Slade, personal communication). In wave B the assessment is made both by the key professional (again with the three scales above) and the patients, who are requested to complete the Lancashire quality of life profile (LQL)[34] and the Verona service satisfaction scale (VSSS).[35–38] Quantitive data on sociodemographic characteristics, psychiatric history, and service utilisation are routinely recorded in the South Verona psychiatric case register. All these data are put into the clinical records and are available on line to clinicians.

The project started in 1994, and about 80% of the patients in contact with the service in that year have been assessed in both waves. Mean time used by the professionals for the assessment was 26.9 minutes for each patient, with a wide range (8–70 minutes), depending on the type of patient and the severity of the conditions.

As an example, summary preliminary data regarding the assessments made in wave B of 1994 are reported. A comparison of results obtained in the group of psychotic patients (those with a diagnosis of schizophrenia, schizotypal, and delusional disorder; affective disorder and organic psychosis) and non-psychotic patients showed, firstly, significantly ($P<0.001$) higher psychopathology in psychotic patients in all items of the brief psychiatric rating scale except in those regarding anxiety and depression; less than 10% had severe symptoms. Secondly, there was significantly (P<0.001) higher disability in psychotic patients in all items of the disability assessment scale, less than 15% had severe disability. Thirdly, there was a trend for higher self reported quality of life in psychotic patients; about 40% of patients reported dissatisfaction with their life. Finally, there were no significant differences in satisfaction with services between psychotic and non-psychotic patients. Satisfaction with South Verona community psychiatric service was high, with a better service performance with respect to professionals' behaviour and manner and a relatively worse performance in the areas of information received and service's access.

These data indicate that in South Verona the diagnosis of psychosis is not necessarily a marker for unfavourable life conditions and that the South Verona community psychiatric service meets the demands of psychotic patients. Moreover, they indicate that the perspective of patients and professionals convey complementary point of views.

Future perspectives

The work in progress in South Verona is aimed at understanding the relation existing between quantitive and qualitative variables and their predictive value on the long term outcome of care. We are trying to identify valid patterns of outcome indicators for specific groups of patients using a multidimensional and multiaxial outcome monitoring as an integral part of patients' care.

In conclusion, we should emphasise that both monitoring and evaluating mental health services using an epidemiological approach require extra financial resources and availability of scientific competence and skills. Before embarking on such a programme its costs and the chances to implement and run it effectively should be carefully evaluated. The advantages of this policy, however, need to be underlined: it makes it possible for mental health professionals to proceed towards ensuring that services are based on empirical demonstration of their effectiveness and to use only treatments that have been proved to be effective; it can also assist the administrators in deciding what programmes are cost effective and whether the mental health system is functioning appropriately.

SCIENTIFIC BASIS OF HEALTH SERVICES

1 Wing JK. The cycle of planning and evaluation. In: Wilkinson G, Freeman H, eds. *Mental health services in Britain*. London: Gaskell Books, 1986.

2 Knudsen HC, Thornicroft M. *Mental health service evaluation*. Cambridge: Cambridge University Press (in press).

3 Tansella M. Community psychiatry without mental hospitals. The Italian experience: a review. *J R Soc Med* 1986; **79**: 664–9.

4 Tansella M, ed. *Community based psychiatry. Long term patterns of care in South Verona*. Cambridge: Cambridge University Press, 1991: 1–54. (Psychological Medicine Monograph Supplement 19.)

5 George LK. Definition, classification and measurement of health services. In: Taube CA, Mechanic D, Adimann AA, eds. *The future of mental health services research*. Washington DC: National Institute of Mental Health, 1989. (DHHS Publication No (ADM) 89–1600.)

6 Tansella M, Micciolo R, Biggeri A, *et al*. Episodes of care in first ever psychiatric patients. *Br J Psychiatry* 1995; **167**: 220–7.

7 World Health Organisation. *The ICD-10 classification of mental and behavioural disorders: clinical depression and diagnostic guidelines*. Geneva: WHO, 1992.

8 Burti L, Tansella M. Acute home based care and community psychiatry. In: Phelan M, Stathdee G, Thornicroft G, eds. *Emergency mental health services in the community*. Cambridge: Cambridge University Press, 1995.

9 Amaddeo F, Bonizzato P, Rossi F, *et al*. La valutazione dei costi delle malattie mentali in Italia. Sviluppo di una metodologia e possibili applicazioni. *Epidemiologia e Psichiatria Sociale* 1995; **4**: 145–62.

10 Balestrieri M, Williams P, Micciolo R, *et al*. Monthly variation in the pattern of extramural psychiatric care. *Social Psychiatry* 1987; **22**: 160–6.

11 Viscogliosi Calabrese L, Micciolo R, Tansella M. Patterns of care for chronic patients after the Italian psychiatric reform. *Soc Sci Med* 1990; **31**: 815–22.

12 Bebbington P, Tansella M. Gender, marital status and treated affective disorders in South Verona: a case register study. *J Affect Disord* 1989; **17**: 83–91.

13 Faccincani C, Mignolli G, Platt S. Service utilization, social support and psychiatric status in a cohort of patients with schizophrenic psychoses. A seven year follow up study. *Schizophr Res* 1990; **3**: 139–46.

14 Lesage AD, Mignolli G, Faccincani C, *et al*. Standardized assessment of the needs for care in a cohort of patients with schizophrenic psychoses. In: Tansella M, ed. *Community based psychiatry. Long term patterns of care in South Verona*. Cambridge: Cambridge University Press, 1991: 27–33. (Psychological Medicine Monograph Supplement 19.)

15 Sytema S, Balestrieri M, Giel R, *et al*. Use of mental health services in South Verona and Groningen. A comparative case register study. *Acta Psychiatr Scand* 1989; **79**: 153–62.

16 Gater R, Amaddeo F, Tansella M, *et al*. A comparison of community based care for schizophrenia in South Verona and South Manchester. *Br J Psychiatr* 1995; **166**: 344–52.

17 Amaddeo F, Gater R, Goldberg D, *et al*. Affective and neurotic disorders in community based services: a comparative study in South Verona and South Manchester. *Acta Psychiatr Scand* 1995; **91**: 386–95.

18 Systema S, Micciolo R, Tansella M. Service utilisation of schizophrenic patients in Groningen and South Verona: an event history analysis. *Psychol Med* (in press).

19 Thornicroft G, Bisoffi G, De Salvia D, *et al*. Urban-rural differences in the associations between social deprivation and psychiatric service utilization in schizophrenia and all diagnoses. A case register study in Northern Italy. *Psychol Med* 1993; **23**: 487–96.

20 Tansella M, Bisoffi G, Thornicroft G. Are social deprivation and psychiatric service utilization associated in neurotic disorders? A case register study in South Verona. *Soc Psychiatry Psychiatr Epidemiol* 1993; **28**: 225–30.

21 Amaddeo F, Bisoffi G, Bonizzato P, *et al.* Mortality among psychiatric patients. A ten year case register study in an area with a community based system of care. *Br J Psychiatry* 1995; **166**: 783–8.

22 Schulberg HC, Bromet E. Strategies for evaluating the outcome of community services for chronically mentally ill. *Am J Psychiatry* 1981; **138**: 930–5.

23 Wright RG, Heiman JR, Shupe J, *et al.* Defining and measuring stabilization of patients during four years of intensive community support. *Am J Psychiatry* 1989; **146**: 1293–8.

24 Jenkins R. Towards a system of outcome indicators for mental health care. *Br J Psychiatry* 1990; **157**: 500–14.

25 Mirin SM, Namerow MJ. Why study treatment outcome? *Hosp Community Psychiatry* 1991; **42**: 1007–13.

26 Attkisson C, Cook J, Karno M, *et al.* Clinical services research. *Schizophr Bull* 1992; **18**: 627–68.

27 Mayer J, Rosenblat A. Clash in perspective between mental patients and staff. *Am J Orthopsychiatry* 1974; **44**: 432–41.

28 Ruggeri M. Patients' and relatives' satisfaction with psychiatric services: the state of the art of its measurements. In: Thornicroft G, Tansella M, eds. *Designing instruments for mental health service research. Part 1. Social psychiatry and psychiatric epidemiology.* Berlin: Springer International, 1994.

29 Ruggeri M, Tansella M. Evaluating outcome in mental health care. *Current Opinion in Psychiatry* 1995; **8**: 116–21.

30 Ruggeri M, Tansella M. Individual patients outcomes. In: Knudsen HC, Thornicroft G, eds. *Mental health service evaluation.* Cambridge: Cambridge University Press (in press).

31 Endicott J, Spitzer RL. The global assessment scale. A procedure for measuring overall severity of psychiatric disturbance. *Arch Gen Psychiatry* 1976; **33**: 766–71.

32 Lukoff D, Nuechterlein K, Ventura J. Manual for expanded brief psychiatric rating scale (BPRS). *Schizophr Bull* 1986; **4**: 594–602.

33 World Health Organisation. *Disability assessment schedule (DAS-II).* Geneva: WHO, 1988.

34 Oliver JP. The social care directive: development of a quality of life profile for use in community services for the mentally ill. *Social Work and Social Review* 1991; **3**: 4–45.

35 Ruggeri M, Dall'Agnola R. The development and use of the Verona expectations for care scale (VECS) and the Verona service satisfaction scale (VSSS) for measuring expectations and satisfaction with community based psychiatric services in patients, relatives and professionals. *Psychol Med* 1993; **23**: 511–23.

36 Ruggeri M, Dall'Agnola R, Agostini C, *et al.* Acceptability, sensitivity and content validity of VECS and VSSS in measuring expectations and satisfaction in psychiatric patients and their relatives. *Soc Psychiatry Psychiatr Epidemiol* 1994; **29**: 265–76.

37 Ruggeri M, Greenfield T. The Italian version of the social satisfaction scale (SSS-30) adapted for community based psychiatric services: development, factor analysis and application. *Evaluation and Program Planning* 1995; **2**: 191–202.

38 Ruggeri M, Dall'Agnola R, Greenfield T, *et al.* Factor analysis of the Verona service satisfaction scale-82 and development of reduced versions. *International Journal of Methods in Psychiatric Research* (in press).

18 Health promotion and disease prevention: the evaluation of health service interventions

DAVID MANT

In 1990, when the United Kingdom government introduced its new health promotion contract for general practitioners, I was one of the first to throw stones.[1] I was angered at the apparent indifference to the evidence assembled by the scientific community, including my own group in Oxford. I argued vehemently that all clinical practice, including health promotion, should be evidence based. I wrote eloquently that health policy should follow research, rather than research following policy.

Over the past five years I have not changed my view on the importance of evidence based policy, but I have been forced to ask myself whether the research community is making life easy for the policy makers. I recently gave a paper in Copenhagen about the role of the medical profession in the prevention of cardiovascular disease. At the end of my typically cautious presentation, someone in the audience asked me an interesting question—could I explain why rates of heart disease were falling when the trials suggested that intervention was ineffective? Wasn't it fortunate that policy makers had ignored the clinical trials?

My reply was that many of the trials of secondary and tertiary prevention have shown intervention to be extremely effective and that implementation of policy based on the results of these trials would make rates fall even more rapidly. But in fact the question deserves a fuller answer. Many of the trials in which I have been involved on the primary prevention of heart disease and cancer have almost certainly been unhelpful to policy makers, not because the results have been disappointing but because the questions they have studied have been unhelpful. This chapter will outline some lessons we can learn from clinical trials of health promotion interventions and will suggest some solutions we might adopt to make them more useful from a health policy perspective.

Lessons from the past

The research and policy perspectives

In 1979 the results of the North Karelia project were published in the *BMJ*. No significant difference in cardiovascular mortality was detected between North Karelia and the control province of Kuopio, but the investigators concluded that the programme had "met its objectives".[3] The reason for this paradoxical statement is shown in figure 18.1, which compares cardiovascular mortality in North Karelia and 10 other provinces in Finland during the period 1971–81. Scientific interest lies in the small difference in slope between the two regression lines—the extent to which mortality fell more in North Karelia than elsewhere. The interest of health policy makers lies in the absolute slope of both lines—the fact that mortality fell dramatically throughout Finland during and five years after the intervention period.

A similar effect was observed in the multiple risk factor intervention trial (MRFIT) in the United States.[4] The difference in cardiovascular mortality between the intervention and control groups (the issue of scientific interest) was again small in comparison with the extent to which mortality in both groups fell

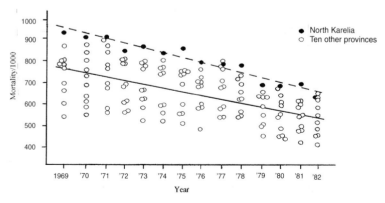

Figure 18.1   Age standardised annual mortality from cardiovascular disease in 100 000 men aged 35–64 years (from Tuomilehto *et al*[3]).

171

short of that predicted at the beginning of the trial (the issue of policy interest). Much has been written to try to explain the reduction in mortality in the control groups in both these trials, but the contribution of the intervention to the observed reduction in mortality in the study population remains a matter of speculation. It is therefore difficult to escape the conclusion that in each case the scientific contribution of the trial to policy making was minimal.

The potential contribution of health service interventions

Much of my own research has focused on the effectiveness of personal intervention by primary care teams in health promotion. One study that does allow assessment of the contribution of personal intervention to a population based health promotion programme is the Stanford project.[5] The intervention was based on a mass media community education campaign in two communities, in one of which (Watsonville) a third of the population were selected at random to be screened and offered individual counselling if they were found to be at high risk of cardiovascular disease. The results are shown in figure 18.2. After two years there was clear evidence of benefit from the mass media programme, but the difference in cardiovascular risk between the

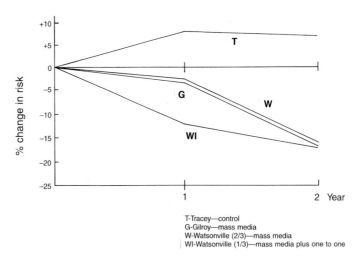

T-Tracey—control
G-Gilroy—mass media
W-Watsonville (2/3)—mass media
WI-Watsonville (1/3)—mass media plus one to one

Figure 18.2 Results of Stanford community education project (from Farquar *et al*[5]).

two intervention communities (Watsonville and Gilroy) and the control community (Tracey) is much greater than the difference between those offered and not offered individual screening and counselling in Watsonville.

A window of opportunity?

One characteristic of NHS health promotion policy has been unrealistic expectations of the effect of personal intervention by health professionals in the context of inadequate public health policy and legislation. This characteristic has been fostered by lack of humility among researchers about the potential of health service interventions to achieve change in relation to other economic and sociocultural determinants of health behaviour. Even if the MRFIT and North Karelia interventions were important in stimulating behaviour change the investigators underestimated the diffusion of health information through the community. This is important because it reminds us that not only should the context of research be defined and described more carefully but the research outcome may also be context specific. The slope of the mortality regression lines shown in figure 18.1 reflects a change in population knowledge and health behaviour. A specific health intervention is likely to be optimally effective at one point on this slope, and there may be a window of opportunity outside which the intervention is ineffective. Figure 18.2 shows that the benefit of the intervention in Watsonville was transient—within two years the control group had "caught up". The length of time during which the benefit of intervention persists depends as much on the rate of change in the control group as on the effectiveness of the intervention itself.

Even the simplest intervention isn't

The most quoted example of effective health promotion in primary care is brief advice on smoking cessation. Russell's seminal paper in 1979 showed that brief advice by general practitioners was effective and set a "black box" paradigm for evaluation of health promotion interventions.[6] In 1988 I helped Diana Sanders and Godfrey Fowler analyse data from a randomised trial of smoking cessation advice by practice nurses.[7] This trial was remarkable for the fact that the intervention was shown to be effective on an intention to treat basis, although only about one in four of the intervention group had received it. Smokers were recruited by their general practitioners, who asked them to see the practice nurse for advice, and the most obvious

173

explanation for the result is that the initial consultation with the doctor was an important intervention in itself. This trial demonstrates that even the simplest intervention isn't. "Brief advice" has at least four components: provision of new information, legitimisation of known information, practical advice on action, and motivation to act. It was the legitimisation element that was most important in general practice in 1988.

Although this experience should have taught me the importance of defining the content of the intervention with painstaking care, we made a similar error in the OXCHECK study.[8] The primary benefit of health checks at three year follow up was a 2% difference in mean serum concentration of total cholesterol between the intervention and control groups. The mechanism for giving dietary advice (the DINE schedule) was meticulously defined but was combined with blood cholesterol measurement. A parallel trial to separate the motivational effect of the cholesterol measurement from the effect of the DINE schedule lacked statistical power to assess an effect as small as 2%.[9] Another parallel trial, that also used the DINE schedule, showed a 2% reduction in serum cholesterol concentration after cholesterol measurement was achieved by distribution of written information without personalised advice.[19] At the end of the day, the key policy question is whether dietary advice in general practice is effective without cholesterol measurement, and we are unable to answer it.

Good methodology, poor questions

I have tried to summarise the lessons learned from the large community trials and from our own work in primary care in the box on page 175. Each point is important in itself, but they can be summarised by saying that the quality of the trial methodology has been high but the questions the research has studied have been poor. We seem to have been assessing black boxes in black holes. But I still believe that effectiveness, and cost effectiveness, can be assessed best in a clinical trial. Is there a solution?

A solution for the future

A methodology of intervention development

The great achievement of the Cochrane Collaboration has been the development of the science of systematic review. Optimal methods of literature searching have been established and quality

Summary of lessons from past health promotion trials

- The potential effect of personal intervention has been over-estimated

- The importance of the social context has been underestimated

- The incentives and barriers to change have not been understood

- The content of interventions has been poorly defined

- The quality of implementation of interventions has not been assessed

- The likelihood that the effectiveness of an intervention is time and context specific (with a window of opportunity) has not been appreciated.

criteria set. The process of systematic review is now recognised to be scientific, to take time, and to be worthy of funding. In health promotion we need to establish a similar scientific methodology of intervention development. As a minimum, this development entails assessment of the incentives and barriers to effective action (by both health professionals and the general population) and clear formulation of the process of change so that objectives can be set and outcomes measured for each stage of the process. In other words, we need to establish a formal methodology for exploring the context of an intervention and defining precisely its content before proceeding to its evaluation.

At present this process seldom happens. Funding is usually available only from the point at which the intervention has been defined and the research question set. I suspect that the process of adequately developing the intervention, and thereby defining the exact research question, should be assigned equal value (in terms of time and funding) to the process of assessing the effectiveness of the intervention. Funding agencies, however, will not support this "pre-protocol" work unless it is seen to be an integral part of the scientific process.

175

Setting minimum quality criteria for funding

One way to encourage intervention development is for funding agencies to extend the minimum criteria used for assessing the quality of any randomised trial. At present, assessment is restricted to methodological issues such as the traditional criteria in the box. My suggestion is that equal weight should be given to the extended criteria and that no trial should be funded unless these criteria have been met. Similar criteria might be adopted in the assessment of trial quality during systematic review.

Extended quality criteria for health promotion trials

Traditional	Extended
Is the randomisation procedure sound?	Is the process of change understood?
Is the proposed analysis on an intention to treat basis?	Are process objectives set?
	Is the intervention well defined?
Is the proposed outcome assessment unbiased?	Is the trial context understood?

Need for multidisciplinary work

To meet these criteria it is necessary to establish a multidisciplinary research team. In clinical trial work the value of health economic input to establish the cost effectiveness of health service interventions is widely accepted. The need for social science input in developing and assessing health promotion interventions needs to be equally widely accepted. In our current trial of secondary prevention of heart disease we have the input of two social science teams as well as a health economics team. The psychologists have been influential in defining and giving a theoretical grounding to the process of change. The qualitative research team has had the role of assessing the incentives and barriers to change and the quality of the intervention at each stage in the process. Both qualitative and quantitive assessments are being conducted in parallel.

Conclusions

This chapter has not sought to undermine the importance of health promotion trials. The influence of trials such as the North Karelia project should not be underestimated. But whereas Russell's study on smoking cessation showed that a simple "black box" trial can be extremely important and influential to health policy, it was as specific for time and place as the intervention it assessed. If we want the results of our trials to influence health policy in the future we must set ourselves the three methodological objectives shown below. As Douglas Adams pointed out, finding that the answer is 42 just prompts another question.[11]

Methodological objectives for the future

- The quality of the question and the quality of the intervention must be as high as the quality of the trial methodology

- Development of the intervention and of the outcome measures assessed must be based on a clear understanding of the process of change established by qualitative research

- Assessment of the overall cost effectiveness of the intervention must be reported in parallel with assessment of the success of the intervention in meeting specified process objectives

---

1 Mant D, Fowler G. Urine analysis for glucose and protein: Are the requirements of the new contract sensible? *BMJ* 1990; **300**: 1053–5.

2 Salonen J, Puska P, Mustaniems H. Changes in morbidity and mortality during comprehensive community programme to control cardiovascular diseases during 1972–7 in North Karelia. *BMJ* 1979; ii: 1178–83.

3 Tuomilehto J, Geboers J, Salonen J, *et al*. Decline in cardiovascular mortality in North Karelia and other parts of Finland. *BMJ* 1986; **293**: 1068–71.

4 Multiple Risk Factor Intervention Trial Research Group. Multiple risk factor intervention trial. Risk factor changes and mortality results. *JAMA* 1982; **248**: 1465–77.

5 Farquar JW, Wood PD, Breitrose H, *et al*. Stanford heart disease prevention program. *Lancet* 1977; i: 1192–5.

6 Russell MAH, Wilson C, Taylor C, *et al*. Effect of general practitioners' advice against smoking. *BMJ* 1979; ii: 231–5.

7 Sanders D, Fowler G, Mant D, *et al*. Randomised controlled trial of anti-smoking advice by nurses in general practice. *Journal of the Royal College of General Practitioners* 1989; **39**: 273–6.

8 Coulter A, Fowler G, Fuller A, *et al*. Effectiveness of health checks conducted by nurses in primary care: final results of the OXCHECK study. *BMJ* 1995; **310**: 1099–104.

9 Robertson I, Phillips A, Mant D, *et al*. Motivational effect of cholesterol measurement in general practice health checks. *Br J Gen Pract* 1992; **42**: 469–72.

10 Neil HAW, Roe L, Goodlee RJP, *et al*. Randomised trial of lipid lower dietary advice in general practice: the effects on serum lipoproteins, and antioxidants. *BMJ* 1995; **310**: 569–73.

11 Adams D. *The restaurant at the end of the universe*. London: Pan Books, 1980.

Index